# AN INTRODUCTION TO REAL PROPERTY LAW

# AN INTRODUCTION TO REAL PROPERTY LAW

**Sixth Edition**

**Alan M. Sinclair, S.J.D. (Michigan)**
**Former Professor and Dean**
**University of New Brunswick**

**Margaret E. McCallum, Ph. D. (Toronto)**
**Professor**
**University of New Brunswick**

**An Introduction to Real Property Law**


May 2012



**Library and Archives Canada Cataloguing in Publication**

McCallum, Margaret E. (Margaret Elizabeth), 1954-
An introduction to real property law / Margaret E. McCallum, Alan M. Sinclair. – 6th Ed.

Includes index.
Order of authors reversed on 4th ed.
ISBN 978-0-433-46961-2

1. Real property--Canada--Textbooks. I. Sinclair, Alan M. II. Sinclair, Alan M. Introduction to real property law. III. Title.

KE625.M33 20 346.7104'3
C20-900623-4
KF570.M3 20

**Published by LexisNexis Canada, a member of the LexisNexis Group**
LexisNexis Canada Inc.
123 Commerce Valley Dr. E., Suite 700
Markham, Ontario
L3T 7W8

**Customer Service**
Telephone: (905) 479-2665 • Fax: (905) 479-2826
Toll-Free Phone: 1-800-668-6481 • Toll-Free Fax: 1-800-461-3275
Email: customerservice@lexisnexis.ca
Web Site: www.lexisnexis.ca

Printed and bound in Canada.

# About the Authors

The late Alan Sinclair was Professor and Dean of Law at the University of New Brunswick, and the originating and sole author of the first three editions of this text.

Margaret McCallum has taught property law to hundreds of law graduates at the University of New Brunswick since she joined the Faculty there in 1990. She is author, with D. Schmedemann and C. Kunz, of *Synthesis: Legal Reading, Reasoning and Writing in Canada*, now in its third edition, and co-author, with Rusty Bittermann, of *Lady Landlords of Prince Edward Island: Imperial Dreams and the Defence of Property*. She is a contributing author, with Jeremy de Beer and Douglas C. Harris, to Bruce Ziff's *A Property Law Reader*, 2nd and 3rd editions, and to Anne Warner La Forest's *Anger and Honsberger Law of Real Property*, 3rd edition.

*Dedicated by Alan Sinclair to*

**Professor Graham Murray**

*Dedicated by Margaret McCallum to*

**her mother, Ruth**
**and her daughter, Emma Ruth**

# ACKNOWLEDGMENTS

The late Alan M. Sinclair described the first edition of this book as "a succinct statement of the basics" of the law of real property. The sixth edition follows in that tradition, and is a continuing tribute to the life and learning of A.M. Sinclair. If the book helps readers to create order from the chaos of real property law, it will have served his purpose and mine.

Thanks to my students at the University of New Brunswick whose questions and comments have prompted some of the changes in this edition. After all these years, it is still fun to teach property law. And thanks to my colleagues, particularly David Bell at UNB, who read and commented on previous editions, and to those across the country who contribute to ongoing conversations, in person and in print, on property questions.

Thanks, too, to the Centre for Advanced Legal Studies, University of London and the Canada Council (for Alan) and the McGill Institute for the Study of Canada (for me) for providing office space and other support during work on earlier editions and to Gian-Luca Di Rocco and Bana Moulhem at LexisNexis Canada.

Margaret McCallum
Fredericton, January 2012

# TABLE OF CONTENTS

# 1

# THE FRAMEWORK OF CANADIAN PROPERTY LAW

This book is an introduction to basic concepts used in the Canadian common law jurisdictions in determining claims about rights and obligations in real property. Resources that the law recognizes as property can be categorized in many ways. For example, the distinction between tangibles and intangibles focuses on whether the property has a physical existence or exists only as an abstract bundle of rights. The distinction between movables and immovables is a rough division between land and non-land. Both of these categorizations are used for various purposes in the common law world, but the basic distinction in common law is between real and personal property. This distinction derives not from the character of the property but from the forms of action that governed civil procedure in mediaeval England.

In disputes over rights in land, the parties could bring a real action, to be put back into possession of the property, called the *res* (Latin for "the thing"). In other disputes over property, the remedy was generally an action for damages — an order *in personam* — made against the defendant personally. Thus, rights in land became known as real property and other property rights as personal property. A leasehold interest, however, was a hybrid. It defined rights in land, but initially, the remedy for interference with rights granted under a lease was an order for damages, not an order to restore the wronged person's possession of the property. As the word "chattel" is another word for "property other than land", the leasehold interest became known as a chattel real.

Even this brief account of why we divide property into real and personal illustrates the relevance to real property of Oliver Wendell Holmes' dictum that "a page of history is worth a volume of logic": *New York Trust co. v. Eisner*, 256 U.S. 345 at 349 (1921). Real property law in common law jurisdictions is a product of its history. It is not a system, planned and implemented in accordance with a coherent vision, but the haphazard outcome of hundreds of decisions resolving individual conflicts over rights and obligations in a particular plot of land. At the macro level, the common law treats land as the basis of the social structure and, in a contradictory fashion, as a commodity to be bought and sold without restrictions. At the micro level, this contradiction is expressed in resistance to attempts by landowners to inhibit free alienation of land by granting the land on conditions that would long outlive the grantor. Some historical background helps in understanding how the law contains and mediates these basic conflicts.

## FEUDAL STRUCTURES

Most of the concepts essential to understanding real property law developed in feudal England. Initially, land rights were determined locally, according to existing custom and the exigencies of each manor. In the Middle Ages, the shift of power from local courts to the King and the centralization of power in the King's court established the authority of common law and legislation. On this foundation, rights in land became more standardized, and, in the developing market economy, easier to exchange. But the function of real property law was not to simplify land transfers. In Canada today, real property law, in its anachronisms and inconsistencies, retains the marks of feudal origins and subsequent struggles to accommodate new social, political and economic realities.

What most lawyers understand by the feudal system is the pattern of landholding imposed on England by William the Conqueror in 1066. Its basic feature is land tenure in exchange for military service. In the aftermath of conquest, the Conqueror became the owner of all the land. As he could not control it all personally, he parcelled it out to 1500 or so barons who supported him. Each baron was allotted a large tract of land to hold (*teneo*) of the King. There was no sale or gift of ownership, as we think of ownership; rather the King granted land to a baron, which the baron held as a tenant of the King. The baron was given, not ownership of the land itself, but certain rights and obligations in relation to the land. In exchange for possession of the land, the baron promised ongoing loyalty and services to the King. The word "feudal" comes from the same Latin root as "fealty", which means loyalty. The grant of land thus confirmed rather than severed the connection between grantor and grantee, by creating obligations that required a continuing personal relationship.

Land is of no value without labour to make it productive, and so, in order to cultivate and defend their land, and to provide the King with the required services, the barons followed the King's example and parcelled out their large tracts to subtenants, in exchange for money and services. One can visualize the developing structure as a pyramid or triangle, with the King at the apex, next a band of barons who are the head tenants of the King, called "tenants *in capite*" and, further down, lesser landholders, called "mesne lords", who owed services to those above them and required services from those below. If the King demanded a supply of men, horses or food from his tenants *in capite*, they obtained them from their tenants, the mesne lords, who in turn looked to their tenants to supply what was needed. At the very bottom were those who had no rights in the land. Property law, therefore, had characteristics of both public and private law — it placed public duties on holders of rights in land, and defined the terms of landholding.

## TENURE

The terms on which tenants held land were called "tenure". As the King's most important concern was defence and waging war, his chief demand was for knights. To be a knight was an honour, and the most honourable form of tenure was knight service, in which a baron or a mesne lord agreed to supply a required number of knights in return for his grant of rights in land. Knight service and other forms of military tenure carried additional obligations, called "incidents". Most of the incidents attached to the predictable but significant events of everyday life. If the lord had children, he could demand contributions from his tenants, called "aids", toward the cost of equipping his eldest son as a knight and his eldest daughter as a bride. Lords could also claim aids for their ransom. Men and women had separate and unequal places in feudal society. Most lords and tenants were men, not women, and the use of masculine nouns and pronouns in describing the rights of landholders is a reminder of the many ways in which one's relationship to land determined one's status.

Today, the power to alienate is considered one of the basic rights of property ownership, but in feudal times tenants could not transfer their rights and obligations with respect to their land without permission of their lord. To obtain this permission, tenants paid the lord a feudal incident called a "fine". Nor could tenants make a will disposing of their real property. On a tenant's death, before the lord would accept the eldest son of the deceased tenant in his father's place, as primogeniture demanded, the son had to pay the lord a sum called "relief". The right of the lord to demand relief applied throughout the feudal triangle, with a variation at the very top, between tenant *in capite* and King. When a tenant *in capite* died, the King claimed the incident of primer seisin, meaning first right to possession. Any new tenant *in capite* had to make new promises of loyalty and pay a sum, in the nature of relief, to enter onto the land.

If tenants died with no one capable of inheriting their property, the lord reclaimed it by escheat. If tenants died leaving children under the age of majority, the lord, by the incident of wardship, became the guardian of the children, able to manage their land and take the profits, with no liability except for "waste", a doctrine to be discussed in Chapter Two. If the child wanted to marry, the guardian had to approve the choice, and the custom developed that the lord would select a person suitable to him — perhaps someone willing to pay the lord for the privilege — and tender this individual as a proper, potential spouse. The ward could refuse only on paying the sum the lord demanded.

These feudal incidents attached only to military tenures. Other possible tenures included "frankalmoign," in which lords conveyed land to the church or other ecclesiastical bodies in exchange for prayers for their souls. Tenants lower down on the triangle held their land in "soccage tenure", which was of low status but, like frankalmoign, carried no feudal incidents. Soccage tenants produced food, fuel and cloth, both to sustain themselves and to fulfil their service obligations to their lords. Some paid rent, and, as money became more significant with the development of a commercial economy, many lords commuted the service obligation to money payments.

Knight service, too, was eventually commuted to a money payment, and even this payment was given up by the end of the 14th century. The commutation of menial and honourable services to money payments made tenure less important, but feudal incidents remained a source of revenue for the lords and the Crown; attempts to avoid liability for incidents produced some of the complications of real property law that remain with us today. The *Statute of Tenures*, 1660 (U.K.), 12 Car. 2, c. 24, passed in 1660, marked a political compromise whereby all lay free tenure was converted to soccage tenure. Henceforth, the majority of landholders held their land by virtue of paying a fixed annual sum called "rent". Over time, inflation reduced the value of the fixed sum, and, as lords gave up collecting it, people lost track of who once held land of whom. The prohibition of subinfeudation, to be discussed shortly, eliminated a great many mesne lords, so that today almost everyone who owns land holds it in free and common soccage tenure directly of the Crown.

Frankalmoign tenure was not dealt with by the *Statute of Tenures*, for earlier statutes, called "mortmain legislation", limited creation of new frankalmoign tenures by prohibiting transfers to corporations or to charities except with special authority. "Mortmain" means literally the "dead hand" and, as corporations do not die, marry or have children, lords objected to corporate tenants since their life cycles offered fewer occasions for exacting feudal incidents. Even today, vestiges of mortmain legislation may create some difficulties in property transfers to corporations or to charities.

Escheat is the other direct survivor of the feudal incidents. The *Statute of Wills, 1540* (U.K.), 32 Hen. 8, c. 1, passed in 1540, gave tenants the right to make a will distributing their real property on death. Today, this right is subject, in some jurisdictions, to legislation protecting family members from being left with nothing. If a person dies without a valid will, a situation called intestacy, provincial or territorial legislation lists the people who are entitled to inherit, in order of priority. Generally, spouses and children have first claim, then parents, then siblings. If a person dies intestate and without next of kin, as set out in the relevant legislation, then the land escheats to the Crown in right of the province or territory in which it is situated. Personal property also reverts to the Crown, but by a different legal theory, called "*bona vacantia*".

Present-day holders of rights in real property are tenants of the Crown, in free and common soccage, as a consequence of the *Statute of Tenures* and the prohibition on subinfeudation, as mentioned earlier. Recall that in the early days of feudalism, tenants could transfer their lands *inter vivos* only after obtaining permission of the lord and paying a fine. This transfer involved substituting the new tenant for the old, and left the various bands in the feudal triangle undisturbed. But an original tenant who did not want to step out of the triangle completely could become a lord of the new grantee while remaining a tenant of the lord above. Instead of substituting the new tenant for the old, they shared rights and obligations in the land. Transfer by this process was called "subinfeudation".

Subinfeudation operated to expand the number of bands in the feudal triangle by introducing the grantee as a tenant of the grantor, who thereby became a mesne lord. Introducing new lord-and-tenant relationships into the space formerly occupied by a tenant alone created difficulties in collecting feudal services and incidents, for the new bands of mesne lords made it hard to determine who owed what to whom. So, through political compromises, the lords obtained passage of the statute *Quia Emptores, 1290* (U.K.), 18 Edw. 1, c. 1 in 1290, prohibiting subinfeudation. By this Act, where T held of L and T then sold to T1, T must drop out of the picture and T1 must hold directly of L. But *Quia Emptores* also recognized the right of holders of estates in land to transfer their rights and obligations to whomever they chose, without first obtaining permission of the lord. Free alienation of land *inter vivos* thus became one of the rights of landholding. Over centuries of land transactions, the L's gradually disappeared and the sides of the triangle got shorter and shorter, with the result that today almost all T's hold directly of the Crown.

## ESTATES

The feudal origins of real property law provide two fundamental property concepts: the Crown owns all the land, and property is a bundle of rights and obligations, recognized and enforced by law. We have seen that real property rights and obligations in England after the Norman Conquest were based on grants made by William the Conqueror. William retained ownership of the land itself, while granting rights in the land to tenants *in capite*. The Crown is still the owner of all the land, in the sense that the Crown retains ultimate sovereignty, and land ownership is still ownership of a bundle of rights and obligations with respect to particular parcels of land. These bundles can be divided into various smaller bundles, called estates and interests, held by different people. Thus, *Quia Emptores* did not end the possibility of several people having different rights and obligations in the same property at the same time, but it limited the ways in which rights and obligations could be distributed.

We can see how this works with a familiar example. If I rent my house to you for a year, we each have certain rights and obligations. You may live there and generally treat the property as your own, but you may not damage it or sell it, and most likely you may sublet it only with my consent. I cannot enter the house except with notice to you, on reasonable conditions. You must pay your rent every month, and give up the house again at the end of the year, or sooner if you do not perform your obligations under our agreement. Thus, we both have different rights and obligations in relation to the property — we could say that neither of us owns it completely, but, since ownership is a bundle of rights and obligations, it is more accurate to say that neither of us possesses the full bundle of rights and obligations that makes up ownership of the house.

It is possible that even together, we do not possess the full bundle, for I may be paying off a loan secured by a mortgage on the house, and my creditor will have rights and obligations under the mortgage. Or the house may be in an area that is designated as a heritage trust area, where legislation prohibits alterations to the exterior of the house without permission of a heritage trust authority. Or the property may be a gift from some ecology activists, who require that I maintain the perennial gardens and plant new trees each year. Additionally, the land may be subject to claims based on aboriginal title of indigenous peoples, as discussed in Chapter Six.

There is nothing very startling in this distribution of rights and obligations, for we have grown up with them. When people describe themselves as owners of real property, we understand that they may not have absolute rights over the property. In modern as in feudal times, property owners must pay taxes. But within the limits set by municipal zoning laws, owners can live on the property, fix up the buildings or tear them down, rent the property, sell it, or give it away. Subject to rights of access for such things as maintaining sewers or power lines, owners can keep others off their property. In short, owners have the right to decide how to distribute the rights and obligations that make up ownership.

Imagine absolute ownership as a complete circle of rights and obligations. As owner, I can divide this circle into various parts. In renting my house, I transfer part of the circle — the immediate right of possession — to you for a defined time, but I retain a large part of the circle that, to use the term of art, is called a "reversion". For the year, we share the circle; I own some rights and you own some rights, in relation to the same property.

The various parts into which I can divide my circle of rights and obligations are called "estates" or "interests". Estates are one of the great inventions of the common law. Another fundamental property concept in the common law world — the division of title into two distinct titles, legal and equitable — comes from the court of equity and will be discussed in Chapter Nine. The concept of estates and the recognition of separate legal and equitable estates permits great diversity and flexibility in the rights that can be created in land, allowing different people to own different rights in the same land at the same time. Limited and particular rights are generally called interests; a fuller part of the circle of rights and obligations that makes up land ownership is called an estate.

The fullest bundle of rights available in land is called a "fee simple estate". In the common law tradition, if we say that O (for owner) owns Blackacre, we probably mean that O owns a fee simple estate in Blackacre. We mean that O is as close as the common law recognizes to having absolute ownership of Blackacre. But we know that the person who rents Blackacre from O, whom we will call L (for Leaseholder) also owns some rights in Blackacre. From now on, then, we will not talk about O owning Blackacre, because we need to be more precise. Instead, we will say that O and L own estates or interests in Blackacre. In the example of L renting Blackacre from O, O owns part of the circle of rights in Blackacre, called a "fee simple estate in reversion", and L owns the rest of the circle, called a "leasehold estate". O owns certain rights and L owns certain rights; together they own the full circle.

In this example, as in all examples involving claims to land ownership in the common law tradition, neither O nor L owns the land itself; each owns rights in or to the land. Recall the feudal triangle, now very flat. At the top is the Crown, owning all the land. At the base is O, holding directly of the Crown, owning a fee simple estate in a specific parcel of land. O may dispose of some or all of the rights and obligations of a fee simple owner, for a defined term or forever, but O's transactions do not affect the Crown's ownership of the land itself.

An estate is a measurement of time, defining how long a person may claim rights in a particular property. There are two classifications of estates at common law: freehold and leasehold. In the mediaeval mind, an estate of indefinite duration was greater than an estate that would end at a definite date, as defined in the lease. It was not the length of the estate that mattered, but the indefiniteness of its termination date. Thus, a grant of rights in land for the duration of a person's life was considered to be a greater estate than a grant of rights in land for 100 years beginning at a precise date, even though the grant of rights for life was almost certainly going to end sooner than the 100-year term. But the latter, because it was a defined term, was a "leasehold estate", while the former was a "freehold estate".

## RECEPTION OF IMPERIAL LAW BY A COLONY

Of course, the nation state that we know as Canada did not exist as a legal or political entity when the people of feudal England were working out these complicated categories of property rights. The British acquired sovereignty over different parts of what is now Canada at different times and by different means; the particular history of each region determined the law that applied when it became a British colony. The British acquired sovereignty over most of what is now Canada by settlement. At international law, that means by taking possession of land that is previously uninhabited, called *terra nullius,* by virtue of having "discovered" it.

An uninhabited land has no existing law, so the settlers bring their law with them — the law of the colonizers is received by the colony. In contrast, if a state acquires new territory by conquest, or by cession of the territory by the peoples who inhabit it, the law in effect at the time of the conquest continues in effect until it is changed by the conquering state, or by the new government established by the conquerors.

These three categories — discovery and settlement of *terra nullius*, conquest, or cession — are not nuanced enough to encompass the range of relationships established between Europeans and the indigenous peoples in lands that became, at one time or another, European colonies. Most of the new lands "discovered" by the European explorers were already inhabited, and so the *terra nullius* theory came to mean that if the indigenous peoples were few in number, and without many of the trappings of European civilization, they could be regarded as having no law. Canadian constitutional scholar Bruce Ryder calls the British claim to sovereignty based on discovery an "ugly fiction" woven into the fabric of Canadian law ("Aboriginal Rights and *Delgamuukw v. The Queen*" (1994) 5 Const. Forum 43).

In 1992, in the context of a claim for recognition of indigenous peoples' land rights, the Australian High Court in *Mabo v. Queensland* (1992), 66 A.L.J.R. 408 (Aus. H.C.), rejected the racist assumption that the Australian continent was a *terra nullius* when the British arrived, and declared that land rights of indigenous peoples, as established by their laws and customs, were not extinguished simply by the arrival of British common law and equity. In Canada, too, as is discussed in Chapter Six, the Supreme Court has also recognized the continuing existence of aboriginal law alongside the law received with European settlement.

Exactly what law is received depends on the date of reception. The date of reception is not necessarily the date that the first settlers arrive in the colony. In some jurisdictions, the date of reception is set by legislation. In British Columbia, it is November 19, 1858. That means that all relevant legislation in force in the United Kingdom at that date became part of the law of British Columbia, and remained part of the law of British Columbia until changed by the legislature of British Columbia. The date of reception in the three prairie provinces is July 15, 1870, the date set for transfer of jurisdiction to the Canadian government from the Hudson's Bay Company, which held the territory by a Royal Charter granted in May 1670. In the absence of a specified date of reception, the date is usually the date that the colonial legislature first met, or the date of royal assent for its first legislation. That gives the older colonies a much earlier date of reception than western Canada. For Nova Scotia, the date is October 3, 1758; for Ontario, which was created out of the old colony of Québec by the *Constitution Act, 1791* (reprinted in R.S.C. 1985, App. II, No. 3), it is October 15, 1792; and for Newfoundland, December 31, 1832.

Québec became a British colony by conquest, in the Seven Years' War. By the *Treaty of Paris, 1763*, France relinquished most of New France and Acadia to the British. By the *Royal Proclamation of 1763* (reprinted in R.S.C. 1985, App. II, No. 1), the British imposed English civil and criminal law throughout its new territories. Civil law for private law matters, including property rights, was re-introduced in Québec in 1774, but not in Acadia, which had been annexed to Nova Scotia. New Brunswick was established as a separate colony in 1784; it treated May 8, 1660 as the date of reception, when Charles II was restored to the throne. For Prince Edward Island, the date of reception might be taken as October 7, 1763, the date of the *Royal Proclamation* introducing English law into Britain's new North American possessions, but courts have assumed that it is July 7, 1773, the date of the first meeting of the Island legislature.

The basics of real property law in England, including *Quia Emptores* and the *Statute of Tenures*, were thus received law in the colonies that became Canada. For greater certainty, the *Constitution Act, 1791* stated explicitly that all future land grants from the Crown in Ontario were to be in free and common soccage. By the same legislation, grantees in Québec could request Crown grants in free and common soccage, instead of in the civil law form.

## PROPERTY LAW AND THE CANADIAN CONSTITUTION

Canada came into existence as a nation state in 1867, with Confederation — the union in a federal state of the colonies of Canada, (comprising Canada East (Québec) and Canada West (Ontario)), New Brunswick and Nova Scotia. The division of legislative powers between the newly created federal government and the governments of the new provinces was set out in the British North America Act (U.K.), 30 & 31 Vict., c. 3, which in 1982 was renamed the Constitution Act, 1867. Under s. 92(13) of the Constitution Act, 1867, the provincial governments have legislative authority over "Property and Civil Rights in the Province". The provinces, which as colonies had received different packages of imperial law, thus had the power to alter that law with respect to property rights. Some provinces have used that power to abolish or significantly amend basic doctrines of real property law, with the result that property law is not uniform across the country. In general, the Canadian provinces have been less bold with legislation restructuring rights and obligations of property owners than was the English Parliament, which enacted radical reforms after World War I, culminating in the Law of Property Act, 1925 (U.K.), 15 & 16 Geo. 5, c. 20.

Although property law is primarily within provincial jurisdiction, the federal government, under s. 91(24) of the Constitution Act, 1867, has legislative authority over "Indians, and Lands Reserved for Indians". In addition, property rights of the Indian, Inuit and Métis peoples are protected under s. 35 of the *Constitution Act, 1982*, being Schedule B to the Canada Act 1982 (U.K.), 1982, c. 11, which states that "existing aboriginal and treaty rights . . . are hereby recognized and affirmed". The term "treaty rights" is defined to include rights in existing or future land claims agreements. Thus, as we will see in Chapter Six, the concept of tenures and estates described above does not necessarily apply to aboriginal title lands, to lands designated as First Nations reserves, or to lands governed by First Nations peoples under comprehensive land claims and self-government agreements.

# 2

# FREEHOLD ESTATES

As we saw in Chapter One, the various Canadian jurisdictions received the English law of tenures and estates, as modified by whatever legislation was in force in England at the colony's date of reception. Because all of the dates of reception were after 1660, Canadian law recognizes only one kind of freehold tenure, free and common soccage. All grants of freehold estates made by the Crown in the common law jurisdictions of Canada are thus grants in free and common soccage. There are three kinds of freehold estates, the fee simple, the fee tail, and the life estate, distinguished from each other by how long they may potentially last.

Freehold estates differ from leasehold estates in that leasehold estates are granted for a definite term of years, whereas freehold estates are granted for a defined but indefinite time. It is not how long the estate may last that distinguishes the leasehold from the freehold estate. Some leaseholds, such as one for a term of 999 years, will be of longer duration than some freeholds, such as one that ends with a named person's death. But because the date of that person's death is not definitely known in advance, the estate is of indefinite length, and hence a freehold estate.

## FEE SIMPLE ESTATES

The fee simple is an estate of inheritance which can be transferred *inter vivos* or by will or on intestacy. In the elaborate language of *Walsingham's Case* (1573), 75 E.R. 805 at 816-17, "he who has a fee-simple in land has a time in the land without end, or the land for a time without end . . . ." Subject always to the ultimate ownership of the Crown, the owner of a fee simple estate owns all of the rights and obligations that make up land ownership, as these are defined by the law of the time.

Under the feudal method of conveyance of a fee simple, which we will look at more closely later in this Chapter, the law required that the grantee be given the land for himself "and his heirs". We think today of O's heirs as those who will inherit the property — people who, on the death of O, are an identifiable and limited group. This is not the meaning of the word as used in determining property rights in feudal times. Originally, the words "to his heirs" meant that the grantee was to receive the property and to keep it in his family until his line of heirs ran out, when it would go back to the lord, the grantor. That is, "heirs" meant the whole line of succession, not particular individuals who would inherit.

But, you might well ask, if the owner in fee simple granted an estate to, let's say, "A and his heirs", knowing that the eldest son would be accepted by the lord as his new tenant on the death of the grantee (A in this case), does not the use of the plural "heirs" mean each eldest son in succession? Did not the grantor intend that both A and his heirs were to share some common interest in the land? No, because if the grantor gave A a fee simple estate, the greatest estate possible at common law, then the grantor gave A all of the rights and obligations that make up ownership, with nothing left over to share. So, with recognition of A's right to transfer estates outside the family, the words "and his heirs" in a conveyance meant simply that the grantee received a fee simple estate.

Hence, there are two distinct parts to the phrase "To A and his heirs", each with a separate function. The words describing the grantee — "To A" in this case, but they could be "to my children" or "to my first daughter to bear a son" or "to all of my grandchildren living at my death" — identify the person or persons receiving the estate. This person is called the "purchaser", regardless of whether the conveyance is by sale, gift *inter vivos,* or in a will. Thus, the words identifying the grantee are called "words of purchase". The rest of the words in the conveyance — here, "and his heirs" — are called "words of limitation". They set limits to the size of the estate; and size, remember, is determined by time. So the words of limitation define the potential duration of the grantee's rights and obligations. "To A and his heirs" thus gave A a fee simple estate — an estate with the potential to last forever, without recourse to the lord.

For many centuries in the common law world, the only words of limitation that would convey a fee simple estate in an *inter vivos* grant were "and his heirs". For reasons that we need not go into here, when the courts were required to interpret testamentary dispositions after the *Statute of Wills, 1540* (U.K.), 32 Hen. 8, c. 1, they recognized grants of fee simple estates without the magic words if they could find a clear intention to grant a fee simple estate. But for *inter vivos* grants, the only acceptable variations on "and his heirs" were "and her heirs" or "and their heirs", or "and heirs". A grant of a fee simple to a corporation, however, was valid without words of limitation, because a corporation enjoyed perpetual succession; in theory the corporation could not die. At common law, failure to use the magic words, in the absence of any other words of limitation, conveyed a life estate.

In the last couple of centuries, most common law jurisdictions have enacted legislation recognizing the validity of the phrase "in fee simple" as alternative words of limitation for creating a fee simple in an *inter vivos* conveyance. More recently, some jurisdictions have enacted further amendments to the common law so that an *inter vivos* conveyance without words of limitation will be interpreted as a grant of all the estate and interest in land that the grantor held. It is important to check the date and content of relevant legislation in the jurisdiction that concerns you, so that you will be able to determine the validity of conveyances that do not use the magic words "and heirs" as words of limitation.

Once it was established that the words "and heirs" in a grant were words of limitation, describing the size of the estate granted, it did not matter whether A or any successors in title failed to produce heirs: the heirs had no rights under the grant anyway. That did not mean, of course, that they could never have rights; after passage of *Quia Emptores* (U.K.), 18 Edw. 1, c. 1 and the *Statute of Wills*, A could give them rights in an *inter vivos* grant or by will.

## FEE TAIL ESTATES

Recall the image of the fee simple as a circle which O can divide with others. With the fee tail, O conveys a part of the circle to A, while retaining a reversion in fee simple if A's estate comes to an end. The word "fee" indicates that the fee tail estate is one of inheritance; that is, it can go to A's heirs. But because the estate is less than a fee simple, the line of descent is cut down (*talliatum*) to the direct descendants of the grantee.

The fee tail began as a conditional fee simple but gained recognition as a separate freehold estate through legislation overturning judicial decisions permitting conveyance of the fee tail estate free of the condition. Just as the words "and heirs" are the words of limitation necessary to grant a fee simple estate, the words "and heirs of the body" are the words of limitation to grant a fee tail estate. Heirs of the body refers to lineal descendants only — it does not include nieces and nephews, for example — whereas heirs alone includes lineal and collateral descendants.

The fee tail could take various forms, depending on the restrictions that the grantor chose to impose. If the transfer was simply to A and the heirs of the body, it was a fee tail general, for the birth of any direct descendants would suffice. But a grant to A and the heirs of his body by his wife, call her S, created an estate, called a "fee tail special", that would end if no children were born in the direct line of descent from A and S. If O wanted the male side of the family to have complete control, O would grant a fee tail male thus: "to A and the male heirs of his body". Similarly, O could grant a fee tail female, or combine a fee tail male or female with a fee tail special.

A grant using the words of limitation "heirs of the body" was a grant of something less than a full fee simple; the grantor was carving out a lesser estate from the full circle of rights and obligations that makes up estate ownership. As with the fee simple, the words "and the heirs of the body" do not give the direct descendants a share in the estate — the words simply identify the duration of the estate that is granted to A, or whomever else is identified by the words of purchase. But because the estate is a fee tail, not a fee simple, A cannot convey a fee simple, only a life estate, for the length of A's life, called, as we shall see, a life estate *pur autre vie*. On A's death, if A has children, the estate goes to them; if A has no children, or if A's direct line of succession dies out in the future, the estate reverts to the original grantor.

Obviously, the condition attached to fee tail estates made them less marketable; attempts to avoid the condition brought courts face-to-face with the contradictions at the heart of property law in the common law tradition. Should a patriarch have the right to tie up land after death, or should conditions be restricted so as to promote the free alienability of land? The courts decided in favour of free alienability, and began to interpret grants "to A and the heirs of his body" as meaning that, once A produced children, A had met the condition of the grant and could convey a fee simple to any one, without restrictions. Patriarchs countered in 1285 with passage of a statute called *De Donis Conditionalibus, 1285* (U.K.), 13 Edw. 1, c. 1, that prevented the conveyance of a fee simple absolute when the grantee had received only a fee simple conditional. The newly defined estate thus created by a grant to A and the heirs of his body became known as a fee tail.

But *De Donis Conditionalibus* did not end efforts to transform fee tails into fee simple estates. Conveyancers and courts connived in developing methods of barring or disentailing the entail through actions involving fictitious parties making fictitious claims. Some of these actions created what came to be known as a "base fee", which could be alienated as a fee, but would revert to the original grantor or his estate if the original grantee's direct line of succession died out. It was not the common law's finest hour, and the details need not concern us here. All the Canadian common law jurisdictions have prohibited the creation of new fee tail estates, and all have provided statutory methods of converting the fee tail to a fee simple. But it is still possible to find fee tails in a chain of title, as well as in English novels.

## LIFE ESTATES

The fee simple and fee tail are both estates of inheritance; that is, they are capable of being transferred. Thus, they have the potential to last forever, subject to whatever restrictions are validly imposed by the grantor by way of conditions. The least of the freeholds, the life estate, is not an estate of inheritance, as it ends with the grantee's death. It is nevertheless freehold because its termination date is indefinite — it is not given us to know the date of our death.

The life estate is created by grant when the grantor explicitly conveys an estate limited to the grantee's lifetime, and by default when the grantor fails to use the magic words of limitation to create a fee simple. Thus, at common law, a grant "to A forever" would convey not a fee simple but a life estate, although some jurisdictions now have legislation stating that a grant, whatever the words of limitation, operates to convey all of the grantor's interest unless the grant shows a different intention. The grantor can best show the intention to create a life estate by saying simply "To A for life". But grantors sometimes use other words of limitation, such as "to reside there for the rest of her life". Because the grantor has not used a term of art, the grant invites arguments over its meaning. It might be a grant of a freehold estate or of a tenancy at will as described in Chapter Four. Or the words might be mere permission to live on the property, which in Chapter Seven you will learn is called a "licence". Remember the various interests in land, and use language that precisely identifies the interest you want to create.

Besides being created by express grant, life estates may arise by operation of law, as when a widower or widow claims the common law rights known as "tenancy by the curtesy" and "dower". The widower, if a child was born alive during the marriage, was entitled to a life estate in any real property owned by his deceased wife. This right was called "tenancy by the curtesy". The widow, regardless of whether children were born, was entitled to "dower" — a right to an estate for the remainder of her life in one-third of any real property in which her husband held a legal fee simple at any time during the marriage. Tenancy by the curtesy and dower have been abolished in the Canadian common law jurisdictions and replaced with protections given under family property and homestead legislation. But married couples, subject to the limits of family property legislation, may create similar estates by wills leaving each other a life estate in the family home, with the property to be shared among the children, or to go to a favoured charity, at the end of the life estate.

## The Doctrine of Waste

With the life estate, as with the leasehold, the holder of the estate in fee simple grants to another some of the rights and obligations that make up ownership. The holder of the life estate, sometimes called the "life tenant" (do not let the terminology mislead you into thinking that the life estate is a leasehold), has the immediate right to possession of the property and to its use as the owner, subject to some restrictions to protect the rights of the person entitled to the property at the end of the life estate. The grantor retains the fee simple in reversion and, on the death of the life tenant, will again have the immediate right to possession. Or the grantor may transfer the fee simple to another by creating a remainder interest after the life estate. In a grant "to my wife for life, then to my eldest daughter and her heirs", the wife receives a life estate, and the daughter receives a fee simple in remainder. In the days when property owners were men more often than women, holders of a remainder were called "remaindermen". Now we call them "remainderpersons". In Chapter Eight, we will look at the common law restrictions on the creation of remainders. For now, remember that a remainder and a reversion are distinct interests following after an estate that is less than a fee simple. The reversion reverts to the grantor; the remainder is transferred to another grantee and so remains away from the grantor.

With the life estate, the rights and obligations that make up ownership of an estate in land are divided between the life tenant and the person entitled to the reversion or the remainder. The life tenant may exclude the reversioner or remainderperson, as the case may be, from physical access to the property, but rights to use and transfer the property are restricted by the terms of the grant and by the common law doctrine of waste. "Waste" as a legal term means action or inaction that permanently alters the land, regardless whether the alteration is for better or worse. At common law, action that improves the land is called "ameliorating waste"; life tenants will not be liable for making improvements, although they cannot force the reversioner or the remainderperson to pay for them. "Permissive waste" is waste by omission — failing to do what a prudent owner would do to maintain the property. Life tenants are not liable for permissive waste, although they are ordinarily responsible for current expenses and routine maintenance, such as cutting the grass and ensuring that snow does not build up and cause damage to the roof.

Life tenants are liable for "voluntary waste" — action that damages the property, unless the grant of the life estate makes the life tenant unimpeachable for waste. It is not voluntary waste if life tenants cut reasonable amounts of wood for their own fuel or construction needs and, in newly colonized jurisdictions in which forests are far-reaching and fields few, life tenants may clear lands for farms. Life tenants may work a mine that already exists on the property, but they cannot open a new one. Even if the grant makes the life tenant unimpeachable for waste, the life tenant will be liable to the reversioner or remainderperson for wanton and severe destruction. Because it was the court of equity that first held the life tenant liable in these situations, by issuing injunctions to restrain the activity, this kind of waste has the peculiar name of "equitable waste".

Since reasonable people might differ on where to draw the line between permissible use, ameliorating waste and voluntary waste (does the concrete wall painted flamingo pink and topped with crushed glass and ribbon wire really improve the property?), the grantor should spell out the respective rights of life tenant and reversioner or remainderperson in the grant. Some jurisdictions have legislation addressing lacunae in the common law doctrine of waste, such as legislation enabling life tenants and reversioners or remainderpersons to compel each other to maintain the property.

## Transferring a Life Estate

As life tenants cannot give any greater estate than the one that they own, the life tenant will have difficulty raising money on the security of the property. What creditor would take a mortgage of an interest in land that would expire with the death of the mortgagor? Likewise, leases of a life estate could be cut short by the death of the life tenant unless the reversioner or remainderperson joins in the lease. Life tenants, can, however, transfer an estate to another that will end with the death of the original life tenant. This estate is called a "life estate *pur autre vie*", roughly translated as a life estate measured by the life of another. It is also possible for the life estate *pur autre vie* to be created directly, by a grant from O "to A for so long as B lives". B acquires no rights in the property by the grant, but is simply there as a measuring life for A's estate, which will end with B's death. In law French, the measuring life is called the "*cestui que vie*".

What happens if the holder of the life estate *pur autre vie* dies before the *cestui que vie*? Suppose A, holder of a life estate from O, grants a life estate *pur autre vie* to B. Then B dies before A. A can take back possession because O's reversion does not come into possession until A's death. But if O transfers to B for the life of A, and then B dies before A, who is entitled to possession? We know O has a reversion in fee simple on the death of A, the *cestui que vie*, but A is still alive. So O has no right to the property yet. A acquired no rights under the grant, and acquires none by B's death. Neither do B's heirs, as the life estate is not an inheritable estate. At common law, then, the first person to drift onto the property could keep it; in a system of relative rights, a claim based on possession will be recognized and enforced by law unless someone comes forward with a better claim based on title. In order to avoid nasty encounters between people wishing to establish themselves as the first to take possession of a tenantless life estate *pur autre vie*, the Canadian common law jurisdictions have made life estates *pur autre vie* transferrable by will or on intestacy.

The life estate brings the contradictory values in the common law into open conflict: how can the law preserve property for the reversioner or remainderperson while allowing the life tenant the greatest economic yield from the property? During England's transition from an agricultural to an industrial/commercial economy, legislation was passed to permit life tenants some freedom to effect conveyances of the property in which they held their life estates that would bind the remainderpersons, generally with court approval. The life tenant could use the income on the proceeds, with the capital held in trust for the remainderpersons, who, at the time of the sale, might be children or as yet unborn. Some Canadian jurisdictions received this legislation when they became British colonies, and some have enacted legislation to achieve similar goals. As with the doctrine of waste, English statute and common law as received in Canada does not adequately respond to problems in this area.

## THE RULE IN *SHELLEY'S CASE*

Until the legislatures deliver us from the Rule in *Shelley's Case* (1581), 1 Co. Rep. 93b, it remains a threat to the peace of mind of law students and practitioners. As distilled from countless confused cases, the rule is this: Where a grant of a life estate to A is followed in the same instrument (will or deed) by a grant mediately or immediately to A's heirs, or heirs of the body, the grant of the remainder is transformed into a remainder in fee simple to the first grantee. By the Rule in *Shelley's Case*, which is a rule of law, not a canon of construction, a grant "to A for life, and remainder to A's heirs" must be interpreted to give A a life estate and also a fee simple in remainder, and the heirs nothing. Put another way, the Rule treats the words "and heirs" as being words of limitation defining the estate that A receives, not words of purchase identifying the heirs as grantees. Of course, the heirs may not be done out of their expected inheritance completely, if A decides to transfer the fee simple to them *inter vivos* or by will, though A has no obligation to do so.

There are two requirements for the application of the Rule in *Shelley's Case*. One we have already seen: an attempt to create in a single instrument a life estate and a remainder in fee simple or fee tail to the heirs of the life tenant. The other requirement will be discussed in Chapter Nine, when we add the equitable estate to the options for creating estates in land. For now, simply attach the following sentence to your statement of the Rule in *Shelley's Case*: the Rule applies only if the life estate and the remainder are of the same kind, that is, only if both are legal or both are equitable.

One further point: where O, by will, conveys land "to A for life and upon A's death to A's heirs", and A is alive at O's death, there is no doubt that the Rule in *Shelley's Case* applies. But if A has predeceased O, it has been argued that, with no life estate in A, the Rule cannot apply. This argument has met with substantial, but not universal, success.

If you have understood the effect of the Rule so far, you may be wondering why we say that A gets a life estate and also a fee simple in remainder. Why not say simply that A gets the fee simple? The answer is that the Rule in *Shelley's Case* will not always operate to give A the immediate fee simple. The words "mediately or immediately" in the Rule mean that the Rule applies even if there is a grant of a life estate in between the life estate to A and the remainder to A's heirs. Thus, if O conveys "to A for life, then to B for life, remainder to A's heirs", B gets a life estate at A's death, and on B's death, A's estate gets the fee simple. There is no limit to the number of estates which might intervene between the life estate in A and the remainder to the heirs; forgetting this fact may lead practitioners to draft grants that the Rule in *Shelley's Case* then transforms into a result very far from that intended by the grantor. Where there is no intermediate life estate, as in the first example, "to A for life, remainder to A's heirs", A will get the immediate fee simple absolute, but only by the combined operation of the Rule in *Shelley's Case* and the doctrine of merger. If the owner of a life estate acquires a remainder in fee simple, the lesser estate (the life estate) is said to merge into the greater (the remainder in fee simple) giving that person an immediate fee simple.

Remember that the Rule in *Shelley's Case* transforms an attempted remainder in the heirs into a remainder in the ancestor. It will apply whenever there is an attempt to give a life estate to the ancestor and a remainder to the heirs — not just in grants using the wording of the two examples given thus far. But the rule applies only if the words in the grant mean the whole line of succession. If there is evidence that the grantor used the words to mean specific heirs, such as heirs of the first generation (the ancestor's children) or some other limited and defined group, then the Rule will not apply. Conversely, if by "children" the grantor meant the whole line of succession, the Rule applies. With the word "heirs" and nothing else, it would be difficult to argue that the grantor meant anything other than an indefinite line of succession, but the singular "heir" might mean one individual. Other words that have raised problems of interpretation include "issue" and "children and their children".

It is still not uncommon, as we have already seen, to grant a life estate to one's surviving spouse and a fee simple in remainder to children or grandchildren. One can do so without attracting the Rule in *Shelley's Case* if one chooses one's words with the Rule in mind. The Rule originated when lords still obtained substantial benefits from the feudal incidents of relief, wardship and primer seisin that might be claimed when property passed by descent on the death of the estate holder. These incidents were avoided if the property passed by two separate grants of a life estate to the ancestor and the remainder to the heirs. The Rule, by denying the remainder to the heirs, ensured that the fee simple estate would pass by descent rather than by purchase.

England abolished the Rule in *Shelley's Case* in 1925. Manitoba did so in 1992. In Alberta, courts have held that the Rule was not part of the received law of the province. In other Canadian jurisdictions, the inclination of practitioners to convey property to A with a remainder to A's heirs may still occasion wasteful litigation.

## THE DOCTRINE OF WORTHIER TITLE

If O devises (makes a grant of real property by will) "to A for life, remainder to A's heirs", A, as we have just seen, gets an immediate fee simple, because of the combined effect of the Rule in *Shelley's Case* and the doctrine of merger. What if O devises "to A for life, remainder to O's heirs"? The Rule in *Shelley's Case* does not apply, because the remainder here is not to the heirs of the person who received the life estate. But because this grant, too, might shield estate owners from feudal incidents, the courts developed the Doctrine of Worthier Title. In a grant or devise of a life estate, followed, in the same instrument, by an attempted remainder to the heirs of the grantor or testator, the attempted remainder is void and the grantor or estate of the testator gets a reversion in fee simple.

Using the example of a devise from O "to A for life, remainder to O's heirs", we would expect, if we did not know about the Doctrine of Worthier Title, that A would get a life estate and O's heirs a remainder in fee simple. Because a will is effective only on the testator's death, we can identify O's heirs. Nonetheless, the Doctrine of Worthier Title transforms the remainder in the heirs into a reversion in O. Again, the heirs lose. The result is the creation of a reversion rather than a remainder.

## SEISIN

Some of you may have wondered about the meaning of the word "seisin" in the feudal incident called "primer seisin". Seisin is the right to immediate possession of a freehold estate. To understand the significance of this definition, we have to distinguish three important real property concepts: ownership, possession and seisin.

One of the rights in the bundle of rights and obligations that makes up ownership is the right to immediate possession. In the absence of a claim based on ownership, the right to possession derives from the fact of physical control. To prevent free-for-alls, the law protects quiet possession, except against a claim based on ownership. Possession does not make you an owner, but in the absence of an owner, gives you rights that no one else can challenge.

With leasehold estates, the right to possession may be separated from the bundle of rights and obligations that belongs to the owner of the fee simple. When O grants a leasehold estate in property that O owns in fee simple, O retains the fee simple in reversion but transfers the right to immediate possession to the leaseholder, L. Although L has the immediate right to possession, L does not have a freehold estate, because L's right to possession is for a definite term — a leasehold. O, who will regain possession of the property at the end of L's lease, or possibly sooner if L breaches some terms of the lease, retains the freehold estate and also seisin. At common law, a leaseholder's right to possession was not seisin because seisin was the right to possession of a freehold estate. O has seisin because O has a freehold estate and the right to possession at the end of the leasehold.

In feudal times, despite L's right to possession, O was the more important person from the lord's point of view because O had sworn loyalty to the lord, and the lord looked to O for feudal services and incidents. And since lords wanted to keep track of who had seisin, at common law freehold estates could be transferred only by a formal ceremony called "feoffment by livery of seisin". Grantor and grantee went on the property where the grantor would pick up a clod of earth or a stone or a tree branch and pass it physically to the grantee, while uttering the appropriate words of conveyance, such as "To A and heirs". The grantor would then leave the land, transferring vacant possession to the grantee.

When only the privileged had the opportunity to become literate, and land transactions were not recorded, the public nature of the ceremony of livery of seisin helped establish the rights and obligations of the new owner in the community where they would be enforced. Indeed, some authors report that grantor and grantee would line up a group of small boys to observe the feoffment ceremony, and at the end each boy would be hit on the head to impress the occasion on his memory — a procedure that is not recommended as an aid to remembering the rules of real property.

A feoffment by livery of seisin operated to transfer the right to *immediate* possession of a freehold estate, and the grantee had to be there to take possession. When livery of seisin was the only way to transfer a freehold estate, no estate of freehold could be created to commence in the future — there could be no abeyance of seisin. But what about all those remainders and reversions? Although, as we shall see, the creation of equitable estates permits conveyancers to do all manner of things not permitted at common law, it is not possible to create a legal freehold estate to vest in interest in the future — an estate that is transferred in the present but in which no rights come into existence until some later time. But one can create an estate that vests in interest at the time of the grant, although enjoyment of the estate in possession is postponed until after the expiration of some intervening freehold estate.

Suppose that O, the owner of an estate in fee simple, promises on January 1st to transfer the fee simple to A on February 1st. If this promise is supported by consideration, A may have some contractual remedies if O reneges on the promise, but at common law, the promise gives A no rights in the land. No transfer of the legal freehold estate will take place without livery of seisin. If livery of seisin takes place on January 1st, the fee shifts irrevocably on January 1st, not a month later, regardless what the parties to the transaction intended. If there is no livery of seisin, there is no transfer of rights in the land. But if O divides the full circle of rights and obligations into two parts, so as to convey one part "to A, for as long as A lives", and the rest "to B and heirs", O has divided the fee simple estate into two freehold estates, a life estate and a fee simple in remainder. O retains nothing, as A and B together have the full circle of rights and obligations that make up ownership in fee simple. Seisin is transferred immediately to the life tenant by a feoffment by livery of seisin, and, on A's death, seisin transfers to the remainderperson, without the necessity for a new feoffment.

Suppose that this conveyance took place on January 1st, and A dies on February 1st. For the month of January, A will own the land, subject to the restrictions on life tenants that we saw earlier. On A's death, B will be entitled to possession of the land and will have all of the other rights that go with ownership of an estate in fee simple. But B has had some rights since January 1st. Since B has been given an estate that is not subject to conditions precedent or contingencies, B's estate vests in interest on January 1st. B knows with certainty on January 1st that the fee simple in possession will be hers when A dies. O has already given it up. Until A dies, B owns an estate called a fee simple in remainder. Although some of the rights and obligations of ownership, such as the right to possession, are postponed until A's death, B already has an estate that can be transferred *inter vivos* or mortgaged or can descend to B's heirs if B dies before A. As we saw with the lease, a person can have ownership rights in property that do not include the right to possession.

But how can B receive a freehold estate on January 1st without a feoffment by livery of seisin? And how can A, the life tenant, transfer seisin to B, because B's right to possession arises only on A's death? The common law recognized the validity of B's future interest (a present estate with possession deferred to the future) if it was preceded by a freehold estate carrying an immediate right to possession. Here, the owner of the fee simple has transferred seisin to A, the life tenant, in a ceremony of livery of seisin. That ceremony suffices for all grants in the same conveyance, no matter to how many grantees. A then takes the seisin for himself, for life, and as a sort of conduit for B.

The life estate in A and the remainder in fee simple in B both vest on January 1st: the life estate vests in possession and the remainder vests in interest, with possession postponed until the end of the life estate. While livery of seisin immediately conveyed the freehold (and the freehold could not be conveyed without livery of seisin), the conveyance divided the circle of rights and obligations between two grantees, neither of whom could exercise the full rights of fee simple ownership: the life tenant will never have them; the remainderperson will have them only at the end of the life estate. Similarly, if O granted a life estate to A and retained the fee simple in reversion, the grant would be effective at common law only with a feoffment by livery of seisin to A, who would take seisin for himself and as a conduit for its return to O at the end of the life estate. Seisin goes to the person who owns the legal freehold estate carrying the immediate right to possession.

One final and very important point to remember about seisin: seisin is a common law concept, and applies only to estates created by common law grants. We call these estates "legal estates", to distinguish them from equitable estates created by conveyances to the uses and recognized by the court of equity. As we will see in Chapter Nine, the rules about seisin do not restrict the creation of equitable interests in land, so long as there is someone seised of a supporting legal estate.

# 3

# QUALIFIED FREEHOLD ESTATES

One advantage of the concept of the estate is its flexibility. We have already seen how O can grant L a leasehold or life estate while retaining the fee simple in reversion. O can also grant a fee simple and retain a reversionary interest, if the grant of the fee simple is conditional on the grantee or someone else doing or refraining from doing something, or on the continuation of certain conditions. Similarly, grantors can grant conditional life estates.

But how can O retain something if O has granted a fee simple — the fullest bundle of rights and obligations in land at common law? To understand the answer to that question, think of what O owns not as a fee simple but as a fee simple absolute — not an egg but a whole egg. If O uses the formula "to A and heirs", A gets a fee simple absolute. O retains nothing and A has everything. But if we have a fee simple absolute, we can have fee simples, or life estates, that are not absolute but conditional. With the conditional fee simple, O grants A something less than the full circle of rights and obligations in the property, for the magic words "and heirs" are followed by additional words of limitation. So the words "and heirs" are given their established meaning, defining an estate that has the potential to last forever, while the additional words of limitation add the potential for an earlier termination.

We have already seen one kind of conditional estate — the fee tail. Conditional fees were commonly used in two other situations in feudal times, and continue to be used so today. First, A may be an ecclesiastical or educational body that O wants to support with a grant of land, but O wants the land back if A ceases to exist or changes its functions. So O will make the conveyance "to A Ltd. so long as the land is used for church/university purposes" (because the grant is to a corporation, the conveyance need not contain the magic words "and its heirs"). Second, O might want to provide for his family but might not quite trust his eldest son. So O might convey "to my eldest son and his heirs so long as he continues to support his aged mother and spinster sisters". Despite some restrictions on the kinds of conditions that are enforceable, the ability to grant a conditional fee simple permitted grantors to exercise the power that comes with landholding, even from beyond the grave.

## DETERMINABLE ESTATES AND ESTATES SUBJECT TO CONDITION SUBSEQUENT

In the struggle to interpret grants of conditional estates, and to allocate rights between the grantor and the grantee, courts came to divide conditional grants into two categories: the "determinable estate" and the "estate subject to condition subsequent", also called the "defeasible estate". Some lawyers argued that passage of *Quia Emptores, 1290* (U.K.), 18 Edw. 1, c. 1, eliminated conditional fee simples where the grantor retained an interest in the land, because that statute forbade subinfeudation and declared that henceforth, in all conveyances of the fee, the grantee would substitute for the grantor, and the grantor would drop out of the feudal triangle. Although it would seem to follow that grantors cannot retain anything when they convey the fee simple, this argument has not found judicial or practical acceptance.

In a grant of a fee simple that is less than absolute, what does the grantor retain? In the grant of a fee simple determinable, the right that O retains is called a "possibility of reverter". With a fee simple subject to condition subsequent, O retains a "right of re-entry" (sometimes called right of entry) for condition broken. These are technical terms and cannot be used interchangeably. Although the two kinds of conditional fee simples appear similar in the form in which they are expressed and in the intentions with which they are created, they are quite different in terms of the legal consequences for both grantor and grantee. To avoid confusion between the possibility of reverter and the right of re-entry, and between these interests and the reversion, in your personal lexicon, link the phrase "possibility of reverter" to the determinable estate, and remember that the two never exist apart from each other. Likewise, link the phrase "right of re-entry" to defeasible estates.

Alas, although the common law is rigid in its compartmentalizing of different estates, there is a dismaying lack of precision in the rules whereby estates and interests in land are assigned to one or another of these two compartments. You may encounter two conveyances where only one or a few words are different, but that difference creates a completely different set of estates and interests. For example, where O makes a conveyance "to A and heirs" and adds a condition whereby if A fails to proceed as directed in the deed then O may take (back) the land, the meaning seems to be the same as in a grant "to A and heirs" for the length of time that certain conditions continue. In the first, O grants Blackacre "to A and heirs but if the land is no longer used for church purposes, then O may reenter and take possession". In the second, O grants "to A and heirs so long as the land is used for church purposes".

Using the words "so long as", O, in the second example, grants a fee simple determinable and retains a possibility of reverter. When (if ever) the land is not used as specified, O or O's estate will get the land back and resume the rights of the owner in fee simple absolute. Using the words "but if", O, in the first example, grants a fee simple subject to condition subsequent; and if A or A's successors in title breach the conditions in the grant, O will have the option of exercising the right of re-entry and taking back the estate. Although O may, in both examples, regain the land, in each both O and A have different estates subject to different rules. With a fee simple determinable and a possibility of reverter, if the conditions on which the grant was given cease to exist, then the grant comes to an end automatically — the fee simple reverts automatically to the grantor, or, if the grantor is dead, to the grantor's estate. But if the estate is subject to a condition subsequent and O has a right of re-entry for condition broken, then O has an option: to re-enter and reclaim the fee simple or to ignore the breach of the condition. If O or O's estate does not exercise the right of re-entry, A will keep the fee simple, which will become a fee simple absolute. We will note other important differences between determinable and defeasible estates as we learn about other real property rules.

Why does a small difference in the words of limitation produce different legal consequences? Because judges in interpreting grants have made a distinction between words that are really indistinguishable in meaning. Does the distinction serve any useful purpose? Legislatures in some jurisdictions have concluded that it does not, and have, by legislation, assimilated these two conditional estates to one, therefore ensuring that contending claimants to the property cannot waste resources in litigation over the grantors' intentions. But grantors lose one possibility for choice.

Attempts to define the difference between determinable estates and estates subject to condition subsequent focus on different ways of thinking about the duration or termination point of the two estates. The determinable estate comes to an end automatically when the determining event is reached — the end of the situation on which the estate was premised. The condition is part and parcel of the grant, defining how long the estate will last. In the absence of other indications of the grantor's intentions, courts have generally interpreted the following words as creating a determinable estate: "while", "whilst", "during", "so long as", "until". These words are supposed to connote a duration or flow of time. The estate flows on, subject to the possibility of reverter. And if the possibility of reverter becomes a reality, the estate has reached its natural, if not inevitable, end. In contrast, the termination of a defeasible estate — one subject to condition subsequent — is considered premature or unnatural. Rather than flowing onto its natural end, the estate subject to condition subsequent is cut short artificially by the grantor's exercise of the right of re-entry. The fee simple subject to condition subsequent is a fee simple with an added condition that may defeat the grant. Words generally interpreted as creating an estate subject to condition subsequent are: "provided that", "on condition that", "but if", "but when", "if it should occur that", "if it happens that".

Although these lists of phrases provide some guidance in interpreting a grant, they are not terms of art that will have the same technical legal meaning in all contexts. Whether a grant creates a determinable estate or an estate subject to condition subsequent is a matter of construction, depending in each case on the intentions of the grantor. The results of this search for the grantor's intentions can seem quite arbitrary; surely if grantors had in their minds the different legal consequences of creating a determinable or a defeasible estate, they would state their intentions clearly using the appropriate technical terms.

The form of mortgage in use in many jurisdictions in Canada today began in the 15th century as a fee simple subject to condition subsequent. A mortgage is an interest in land created to secure payment of a debt. In the typical modern mortgage, the borrower transfers a fee simple estate to the lender, subject to the borrower's right to re-enter on payment of the debt. At common law, the terms of this condition were construed strictly, and borrowers often lost the right to regain their property for trivial defaults on their payment obligations. The court of equity, however, began to provide borrowers with some relief against loss of their estates. The rules governing modern mortgages are a compound of common law rules regarding estates subject to condition subsequent, rules of equity concerning the borrower's interest, which came to be known as the "equity of redemption", and legislation.

As noted above, grantors may attach conditions to life estates as well as fee simples, if the grantor wants to control not only the disposition of the property on the life tenant's death, but also the life tenant's behaviour or use of the property. Grantors of life estates to widows sometimes require the widow to remain faithful to the dead spouse. In a devise "to my widow for life so long as she remains unmarried", the widow receives a determinable life estate, with two natural termination points: her death, or her remarriage, whichever comes first. The grantor's estate has both a possibility of reverter and a reversion in fee simple. If the widow remarries, the possibility of reverter becomes a reality and the estate immediately reverts to the grantor's estate. Otherwise, the estate reverts to the grantor's estate at the widow's death. Similarly, a devise "to my widow for life providing she does not remarry", creates a life estate subject to condition subsequent. Here, the natural termination point of the life estate is the death of the widow, but because of the condition added to the grant, the widow, if she remarries, faces the prospect of having her life estate cut short by the executor of the grantor's estate choosing to exercise the right of re-entry.

As we have seen, small differences in wording may produce quite different legal consequences. The requirement for the magic words "and heirs" to grant a fee simple was relaxed for devises. Suppose, then, that O, as a testator, devised Blackacre to his widow, as long as she remained such. Had O intended to give his widow the fee simple or merely a life estate, determinable in either case? As often happens when courts must divine the grantor's choice when the grantor probably had not realized that a choice was necessary, the decided cases are difficult to reconcile. Such ambiguity should be avoided by using technical language and using it correctly.

## GRANTS SUBJECT TO CONDITION PRECEDENT

Before leaving the subject of conditional estates, a warning: be careful to distinguish between wording in grants that imposes a condition for keeping an estate and wording in grants that creates a condition for getting the estate in the first place. For example, a grant "to A and heirs providing A is 21" is not, as you might suppose, a fee simple subject to condition subsequent but a grant to A that is conditional on A reaching the age of 21 within the time limit allowed by various real property rules. In some contexts, we might call this grant a contingent remainder. There is a contingency that A must meet — being 21 — before A will get any estate under this grant. We can also say that the grant is subject to a condition precedent. A has no estate unless she meets the condition, but if she meets the condition within the required time, she gets a fee simple absolute. Reaching the age of 21, a state that, by definition, cannot continue, is not a condition that she has to maintain in order to keep her estate.

In drafting or interpreting conditional grants, you must think very carefully about the meaning and possible ambiguities of all words in the grants, because the same phrase can have different meanings, depending on the context. Take for example a grant "to A and heirs providing she is Prime Minister of Canada". We have here the magic words of limitation to create a fee simple, but what kind of fee simple? Is being Prime Minister a condition precedent, a condition subsequent, or both? If A becomes Prime Minister, is the fee simple estate hers henceforth, or will she lose it when she loses her office? Rather than litigating these questions, eliminate possible sources of ambiguity before your clients sign a document you have drafted.

## INVALID CONDITIONS

As we will see in Chapter Ten, if a grant contains a condition that violates the Rule against Perpetuities, the condition is invalid. Courts will also strike down conditions that create undue restraints on alienation, that offend against public policy, and that are uncertain. As well, in most jurisdictions, human rights legislation prohibits terms in agreements of purchase and sale of land, or terms in leases, that discriminate on the basis of grounds set out in the legislation. These vary from jurisdiction to jurisdiction, but generally include race, colour, religion, national origin, ancestry, place of origin, age, physical disability, mental disability, marital status, sexual orientation and sex. We will not pause to examine the multitude of cases on invalid conditions, but they are another reason for practitioners who are drafting conditions to choose their words carefully.

The legal consequences of a finding that a condition is invalid depends on the kind of estate the grant created. In grants subject to condition precedent, in which the potential grantee gets nothing until the condition is met, the grant fails completely if the condition is invalid. With determinable estates, the same result follows, although for a different reason. Since the condition in a determinable estate is considered to be an integral part of the words of limitation defining the duration of the estate, the grant is invalid and the grantee receives nothing if the condition is invalid. In contrast, because the estate subject to condition subsequent is conceptualized differently — as an estate with a condition added — an invalid condition is severed from the grant and the grantee receives an absolute estate.

# 4

# LEASEHOLD ESTATES

The feudal concepts that we use to describe land ownership are familiar to us in the non-freehold context, where the phrase "landlord and tenant" is still part of everyday vocabulary. In this chapter, we look more closely at the leasehold estate, the estate that has a limited duration and a definite termination date. From the discussion of seisin in Chapter Two, you know that owners of leasehold estates, while entitled to possession for the duration of the lease, are not seised of their estate. Seisin remains with the owner of the fee simple in reversion. But leaseholders have ownership rights; they own a chattel real. Recall the discussion in Chapter One of the basis of the distinction between real property and personal property. Because it was the landlord, not the leaseholder, who had seisin, only the landlord could bring a real action demanding that a wrongful possessor give up the property. The leaseholder was limited to an action for damages. Although legislation has long since abolished these restrictions on remedies, we retain the property categorizations and terminology derived from them. The chattel real is an estate in land that is classed as personal property.

There are four kinds of leaseholds: the fixed term, the periodic tenancy, the tenancy at will and the tenancy at sufferance. As we examine each in turn, we will see that the definition of the leasehold as an estate with a definite termination date encompasses considerable variety.

## THE FIXED TERM

If O conveys to A for a term of one week, one month, one year, 99 years, or even 999 years, O retains the reversion in fee and A acquires the right to sole possession under a leasehold for a term of years. Unless otherwise provided in the lease, the estate ends automatically on the expiration of the agreed-on term; renewal requires negotiating a new lease agreement. In a fixed term tenancy for a period of one year, it is common to have the rent paid every month. Similarly, in a fixed term tenancy for a period of several years, rent is often paid yearly, and the lease may include provisions for annual increases.

## THE PERIODIC TENANCY

The periodic tenancy is also called a tenancy from year-to-year, month-to-month, or week-to-week, as the case may be. These names suggest the way in which this leasehold differs from the fixed term. The time units that define the tenancy — weeks, months, or years — are but portions of the entire tenancy; the tenancy renews automatically at the end of each period unless the landlord or tenant gives timely notice of non-renewal. Under the provisions of some leases, and some residential tenancies legislation, fixed term tenancies are converted to periodic tenancies on expiration of the fixed term.

At common law, the notice required to terminate a periodic tenancy is the length of the tenancy period, but the lease itself may provide for a different notice provision. The date on which notice, to be effective, must be communicated will depend on the tenancy period; missing the deadline by even an hour could result in being obliged to pay rent for a full period beyond what one wished. For residential tenancies, most of the Canadian jurisdictions have enacted legislation defining notice periods and providing tenants with some security of tenure. Under the relevant legislation, landlords may have to give more notice than do tenants, or the notice period may differ depending on the reason for terminating the tenancy.

## THE TENANCY AT WILL

A tenancy at will has no set period and continues at the will of both landlord and tenant; either may terminate it by notice. Tenancies at will may be created if the vendor of a property permits the purchaser to move in prior to closing, or if a landlord permits a prospective tenant to move in, leaving the terms to be arranged later. The tenancy may be terminated expressly, by either party so informing the other, or involuntarily when either party dies or even when the landlord sells the reversion to a third party. In addition, statutes of limitations in most jurisdictions provide that a tenancy at will terminates automatically at the end of one year. Because of this provision, if a person comes into possession of land with the permission of the owner, possession beyond one year without a renewal of the permission may form the basis for a claim in adverse possession, as discussed in Chapter Five. In most jurisdictions, accepting rent for fixed periods — by the month, for example — will convert the tenancy at will into a periodic tenancy, requiring notice for termination.

## THE TENANCY AT SUFFERANCE

As the name of this leasehold suggests, it is based on forbearance. Because it is the landlord who ordinarily enjoys more power in the landlord-tenant relationship, it is the landlord who forbears or suffers. A tenancy at sufferance arises when the tenant remains in possession, without permission, after expiration of the term in the original tenancy. As with the tenancy at will, if the landlord continues to accept rent the tenancy is converted to a periodic tenancy, with terms as close as possible to those of the expired agreement, including notice provisions.

## FORMALITIES OF CREATION

A lease should identify the premises, the parties, the term, the date of commencement, the rent, the allocation of responsibility for utilities and ongoing maintenance, and any other terms that the parties have negotiated. Residential tenancies legislation may provide for some standard or minimum terms that are part of residential lease agreements. Oral leases in some circumstances create enforceable rights and obligations, but legislation governing registration of interests in land may provide that leases for terms of more than a specified number of years must be registered on title in order to bind subsequent purchasers.

The *Statute of Frauds, 1677* (U.K.), 29 Car. 2, c. 3, enacted in England in 1677, is part of the received or enacted law in Canadian common law jurisdictions. It provides that unless a lease of over three years is in writing and signed by the landlord, it creates a tenancy at will rather than a fixed term tenancy; and as noted earlier, acceptance of rent by the landlord will convert a tenancy at will into a periodic tenancy.

At common law, tenants are entitled to assign or sublet their leasehold, subject to any restrictions in the lease agreement. In an assignment, the tenant gives up the entire balance of the term. A transfer of rights under the lease for any period less than that, even if for only a day less than the full term, is a sublease. Residential tenancies legislation may define the circumstances in which landlords must permit tenants to assign or sublet their leasehold. Provisions in commercial leases can be quite complex and restrictive, permitting the landlord considerable control over the use of the property during the leasehold.

# 5

# OWNERSHIP, TITLE AND THE LIMITS OF OWNERSHIP

So far, we have been considering ownership of property as ownership of various bundles of rights and obligations, called interests or estates. Estates define the temporal limits of ownership — how long we can exercise our rights. Now we turn our attention to the physical limits of ownership — the extent of the estate in space. We also consider how owners can protect their ownership rights by registering their title, and how they can lose their rights by failing to assert them in a timely fashion. Finally, we look at the power of the state to redefine the bundle of rights and obligations that makes up estate ownership, through zoning or other legislation that restricts owners' rights to use the land in whatever way they choose.

## PHYSICAL BOUNDARIES AND INHERENT RIGHTS OF OWNERSHIP

### Water

Draw a sketch of a piece of property, roughly rectangular in shape, owned by O. On its southern border it faces the sea and the waves of the ocean pound on its beach. The eastern border is marked in part by a stream, flowing from adjoining land, owned by A. The stream turns and flows across O's land, emptying into the ocean. A creek where it enters O's land, the stream grows quickly and becomes a river affected by the tides as it approaches the sea. From the north a subterranean stream flows southward, its destination unknown. On the west there is a lake that forms part of the boundary with the land of B, the whole of the lake being contained within the boundaries of O's and B's property. A natural pool or pond of water lies completely within O's boundaries, and lying under the property is groundwater that supplies O's well. Consider now the issues that these various bodies of water raise for O, A, B, and the general public.

Let's begin with the ocean. While in most cases in Canada we have the right to walk on an ocean beach, we do not have the right to cross O's land to get there. So where does O's land end? The general rule for interpreting grants of property bounded by tidal waters is to presume that the boundary is the average high-water mark. Below that line, to seaward, the foreshore (the land between the high-water mark and the low-water mark) and the bed of the sea belong to the Crown. The Crown may grant rights in the foreshore or even the ocean bed, but absent an express grant of the foreshore, O cannot prevent people from walking on the foreshore and O cannot erect structures there to enhance his or her access.

Consider now the stream that marks part of the eastern boundary of O's property. Land along a river is called riparian land, and the owner of land along a river is a riparian owner. Grants of land along a river may describe the physical boundaries of the parcel being granted as extending to the water's edge, and following the bank of the river in its various courses. At common law, the interpretation of these words depended on whether the river was tidal or non-tidal. With a tidal river, as with the ocean, a grant to the water's edge granted ownership rights only to the high-water mark, in the absence of words in the grant showing a different intention. With non-tidal rivers, the same words were interpreted as granting ownership rights to the bank of the river and also the river bed. Where a single owner owned both banks, that owner would own all of the river bed. Where the river flowed between properties of two different owners, each would own the river bank on his or her side, and the river bed to the middle thread of the river — *ad medium filum aquae*, in the Latin phrase often cited in the cases. The middle thread of the river is an imaginary line drawn down the main channel of the river.

In England, where courts developed these presumptions about the meaning of words used to describe land boundaries, tidal rivers were generally navigable and non-tidal rivers were generally non-navigable, at least by commercial craft. In North America, the situation is quite different. The Europeans who first explored what we now call Canada used the river systems as their highways into the interior of the continent. These great rivers, although tidal at their mouths (think of the famous Reserving Falls at the mouth of the Saint John River in New Brunswick), remain navigable long past the point at which they are no longer tidally influenced. In Canadian law, then, the tidal/non-tidal distinction gave way to a navigable/non-navigable distinction.

The distinction between navigable and non-navigable is not a precise one; courts have held that a river is non-navigable even if it is navigable by small recreational craft, or is suitable for transporting rafts of timber. As well, courts have held that rivers are navigable even if navigation is interrupted at discrete points by rapids or water falls. Generally, Crown grants of land along a non-navigable river are interpreted to grant ownership of the river bed to the middle thread of the river, unless the words of the grant or relevant legislation preclude that interpretation. However, very few riparian owners today have ownership rights in the beds of rivers flowing along or through their lands, as most jurisdictions have enacted legislation providing that the Crown owns river beds and also a buffer strip of land between the water's edge and lands granted to a private owner.

Ownership of part of the river bed gives the owner the exclusive right to fish in the waters flowing over that part. This right, called a profit of piscary, is a real property right of the kind known as a *profit à prendre*, which we will consider in more detail in Chapter Seven. Although the profit of piscary derives from ownership of the river bed, it can be severed from that ownership and transferred to someone else.

Regardless who owns the river bed, riparian owners do not own the water in the river flowing along or through their property; instead, they own rights to use the water, sometimes referred to as usufructuary rights. In our example, both O and A are riparian owners of the stream that separates their properties. A's land is upstream of O's, meaning closer to the source of the stream, and so A is an upper riparian owner with respect to O, and a lower riparian owner with respect to the owners further upstream. As an upper riparian owner, A has access to the water before O does. What happens if A takes so much of the water that there is not enough left for O, or if A pollutes the water so that it is no longer of any use to O?

At common law, the definition of riparian rights contained some inherent limits that minimized the likelihood of conflicts over the quantity of water that riparian owners could take from rivers flowing along or through their property. Riparian owners could take as much water as they needed, even if their doing so interfered with the water available downstream, but only for ordinary domestic purposes connected with their riparian land. By interpreting ordinary domestic purposes quite restrictively, for example, as water for a few cows but not for a commercial herd, judges balanced the needs of upper and lower riparian owners. Riparian owners could take water for extraordinary uses beyond the everyday needs of an ordinary household only if such use did not interfere with rights of lower riparian owners to have the river flow past undiminished in quality and quantity.

Discharge of waste material from household or industrial activity into a watercourse may also interfere with the riparian rights of downstream owners. Under the common law regime, if a downstream owner could prove that the activities of an upstream owner altered the quality of the water flowing through or past the riparian lands, the downstream owner could obtain an injunction to stop the activity. It was not necessary to prove actual damage, as any interference with riparian rights was actionable in order to prevent the upstream owner from continuing the activity long enough to be able to claim to have acquired the right to continue it.

Judges developed the law of riparian rights in England at a time when water use was limited by the technology for extracting it, and clean water was relatively abundant. At common law, the rights of lower riparian owners limited the rights of upstream owners to divert water from the river, to dam the river, or to use it to carry away agricultural or industrial wastes. Governments that considered these activities as necessary for economic development cleared the way for them by legislation expropriating riparian rights, or by limiting the remedy to damages rather than an injunction — in effect, sanctioning a forced sale of the downstream owners' rights to the upstream owner. More recently, governments have created specialized agencies to regulate some of the activities that contribute to environmental degradation.

The discussion so far has focused on waters that flow in a defined channel across the surface of the land. What about the subterranean stream in our example? If it flows in a defined channel, the owners of the land through which it flows have the same rights to its use as they would with a similar stream on the surface. But if the underground water is not in a definite channel — sometimes a difficult factual determination — then the water is "percolating water", and different rules apply. Groundwater is also percolating water. Some analogy has been made between percolating water and wild animals or fish, which cannot be owned until captured. Certainly at common law, no one owns percolating water in an underground reservoir. But if O can extract the percolating water and bring it to the surface, O can claim ownership rights in the water, even if it is established that the water actually comes via subterranean channels from a reservoir under adjoining land.

With the growth of relatively high density communities in unserviced areas, with wells for each lot, conflicts over use of percolating water are not satisfactorily resolved by the common law's "first capture" approach. In many jurisdictions, particularly where water shortages are common, legislation sets limits on how much groundwater an individual can extract. In the absence of legislation, excessive use may be curbed by tort actions in nuisance or negligence if the use has caused foreseeable harm to a neighbour.

Now consider the two remaining bodies of water on O's property — the lake lying on the boundary and the pond lying completely within O's boundaries. Both will be treated for most purposes as a flowing stream in that both O and A have rights of riparian owners to use the water in an equal and reasonable fashion and neither will own the water. With the pond that is entirely on O's land, O's use of the water will not be limited by the rights of lower riparian owners, since there is no stream draining onto another's land. It is unlikely, however, that either A or O can claim ownership of the bed of the lake. In most jurisdictions, lake beds are reserved to the Crown. If that is the case, absent legislation or an express provision in the grant, a grant of property on a freshwater lake that describes the property as extending to the bank or shore or to the water's edge is interpreted as meaning that the property extends to the low-water mark. If the lake or pond has been created (artificially) by the construction of a dam, the middle thread of the original stream remains the boundary, unless legislation or the wording of a deed provides otherwise.

There is another category of water besides riparian or percolating: surface water draining naturally across the land, but not in a defined channel and not all of the time. The older cases talk of water that squanders itself across the land. Just as with the distinction between riparian and percolating water, the distinction between riparian and surface water is a question of fact, to be determined in each case on the evidence. With surface water, the issue is more likely to be who has responsibility for the damage it causes rather than who can use it. The basic common law approach is to treat the water as a common enemy, with individual property owners free to take steps to protect their land from flooding. Owners may retain surface water on their property if they wish, as their neighbours lower down have no right to receive it. Owners may also put up barriers to keep the water from coming on their own property, but they cannot create artificial channels to direct it onto their neighbours' property. Whether erecting a barrier also creates an artificial channel may be a difficult factual determination. In contrast to the common law, the civil law doctrine in Québec (adopted by Alberta on this point) requires properties that stand in the natural flow of surface water to allow the water to follow its natural flow — one can neither hoard the water nor put up barriers against it. More generally, legislation often assigns responsibility for flood control to the entity that controls the relevant water systems.

## The Subsurface

In mediaeval times, when many people thought of the world as flat, the physical limits of property ownership were expressed in a Latin maxim — *cuius est solum, eius est usque ad caelum et ad inferos* — roughly translated as "who owns the fee in the surface owns not only that surface but up to Heaven and down to Hell". Generally, when we think of the physical dimensions of a fee simple, we think of two dimensions — length and width. But sketch a cutaway section of the earth so that you see the surface of O's land as well as the subsurface. Now imagine two fee simple estates, one on top of the other, one in the surface and the other in the subsurface.

At common law, it is possible for O to grant a fee simple in the subsurface so that surface and subsurface are owned separately. Generally, if O owns the fee simple absolute in Blackacre, O owns the subsurface unless the chain of title shows that it was reserved or conveyed separately at an earlier date. But holding title to the subsurface does not mean that O owns everything that lies therein, for at common law the Crown is entitled to precious metals and to treasure trove — gold and silver that has been refined and then hidden on the land by persons unknown. In addition, most Crown grants reserved ownership of minerals, coal, and petroleum hydrocarbons for the Crown. In the early years of settlement in the prairie west, the federal government's land grants to the Canadian Pacific Railway, as well as to early settlers, did not reserve mineral, coal, or petroleum hydrocarbons for the Crown. In western Canada, then, there is a mixture of Crown-owned and privately owned mineral rights. The latter are called freehold mineral rights, and can be conveyed in the same manner as a fee simple.

Whatever one owns, the rights of ownership are never absolute but are limited by the owner's obligations to others. To your cutaway sketch of O's property, add on each side the property of O's neighbours, A and B. And give the subsurface under O's land in fee to C. Where O's land is in its natural state, that is, unencumbered by buildings or structures, then O has a right at common law to receive lateral support from the lands of A and B. It follows therefore that if A excavates for a foundation with resulting subsidence on O's lot, A will be liable to O for the cost of restoring the surface. To put this in a slightly different way, landowners have an absolute right to have their land supported, in its natural state, laterally by land of their neighbours. Note that the words used are "absolute right". There is no question of how careful A or B might have been or how unpredictable the subsidence was: non-negligence is not a defence. Note, too, that the right to support may impose a limit on the right to extract percolating water, discussed above. If you take so much water that you empty an underground reservoir that was supporting your neighbour's surface, you may be liable for any resulting damage.

Now place a building on O's land, while A's and B's are unimproved. The right to support that is inherent in estate ownership applies to the land only, not to buildings on the land. It is possible to secure a right to support of a building through an easement, an interest in the land of another to be discussed in Chapter Seven. But assume that O has no such right here. And suppose that B excavates and O's land subsides, damaging not only the land but the building as well. Is B absolutely liable for all of this damage, part of it, or none of it? Since B has no obligation to support O's building, we have to know whether the land would have subsided even if O's building was not there: was the subsidence caused only by B's removal of support or was the weight of the building a contributing cause? Since this is a counterfactual question — what if the building had not been there? — the answer can be expressed only in probabilities. And it is here that evidence of non-negligence may be relevant. O will say "my building stood for 25 years without a problem, then B excavated and the land subsided. *Res ipsa loquitur*." O may also bring in expert witnesses who will criticize what B did and suggest what B should have done. That will shift the evidentiary burden to B, who will bring in expert witnesses to testify as to B's reasonable precautions to shore up and backfill properly, so that the subsidence must have been from the weight of the building, not the excavation. Then the judge must assess whose explanation of the subsidence is more persuasive, on the balance of probabilities. If it is O's, B will be liable for the damage to the land and to the building as well, since damage to the building is consequential to the damage to the land and therefore recoverable.

Look again at your sketch. O has one other neighbour besides A and B — C — who owns the fee simple in the subsurface below O's property. C must provide O with subjacent support. Suppose that C, perhaps in mining coal, has removed so much of the subsurface that the surface has subsided. Where there has been subsidence following subsurface mining, the surface owner may rely on a presumption that the mining activities caused the subsidence, regardless of the presence of buildings on the property. The evidentiary onus then shifts to C to rebut the presumption. C may do so by introducing evidence that the mining activity was carried out in such a way as to maintain support for the surface, or by introducing evidence that O's activities on the surface would have caused the subsidence, even without the mining activity.

Just as O may bargain with neighbouring landowners for the right to support of buildings, so C may acquire from O a release of O's inherent right to subjacent support. In mining areas, where mining companies have acquired the full fee simple and then sold the surface, the deeds may contain a clause reserving to the mining company the right to cause subsidence without liability.

## Airspace

Although humans throughout history have been fascinated by the airspace above them, it is only in the last couple of centuries that they have been able to make much use of it. In modern times, conflicting use requirements have led to both judicial and legislative repudiations of the extent of ownership suggested in the Latin maxim *cuius est solum, eius est usque ad caelum et ad inferos*. Property owners cannot claim damages for trespass from aircraft flying through "their" column of airspace at 30,000 or 40,000 feet. But they can claim damages from the owners of overhanging buildings, fences or even trees, unless their owners have obtained an easement giving them the right to use their neighbour's airspace.

Where, in between the high-altitude plane and the overhanging apple trees, do O's rights disappear? It is physically impossible to draw a line at 1,000 feet or any other such "reasonable" distance so we resort to what is reasonable in the circumstances. O has the rights necessary to make reasonable use of the surface property and the airspace that can be controlled from that property. The owner of a fee simple can convey a fee simple in the airspace above the surface, just as he or she can convey a fee simple in the subsurface. Some jurisdictions have legislation providing standards for surveyors and conveyancers to use in writing descriptions for deeds to empty air space, or for use in planning, developing and selling condominium units in high-rise towers. Some municipalities use height limitations to restrict building density; these municipalities may permit the owner of a low-rise building to sell the unused development rights to empty airspace above the building to the owner of a nearby parcel of land. By combining the development rights transferred from the first parcel with the development rights for the second parcel, the owner of the second parcel is able to build something higher than otherwise permitted.

Owners of property do not have the right to prevent others from erecting structures that will block their light or interfere with their view, unless they have acquired the right to the light or view by way of easement. In some jurisdictions, zoning by-laws may limit construction that will interfere with a view from a public park or civic landmark, but that is a different matter. Whenever there is a question about the inherent rights of estate ownership or the physical extent of property rights, remember to check for legislation that adds to or amends the common law.

## FIXTURES

As discussed in Chapter One, in the common law world, freehold estates and most other interests in land are categorized as real property, and all other property, including leasehold estates, are categorized as personal property. A building on land is generally treated as part of the land itself; thus, when one buys a house on a city lot, or a farm property complete with house, barns and implement sheds, the legal description of the property identifies the boundaries of the land, but does not itemize the buildings constructed on the land. For those who like Latin maxims, the relevant one is *quicquid plantatur solo, solo credit* (that which is attached to the soil becomes part of the soil). Goods, known in legal parlance as chattels, may also become part of the land, if they are attached to the land or to structures that are considered part of the land so as to become fixtures.

In determining whether an item has sufficient attachment so as to become a fixture, judges ask whether a reasonable person, looking at the degree and purpose of the attachment, would conclude that the item was intended to become a permanent part of the land. Items that are securely and permanently attached to land or a structure on the land in order to make better use of the land become fixtures. The word "permanently" must be understood not as meaning "forever" but as meaning "for as long as the item serves its purpose of enhancing the value or the usefulness of the land".

Because the categorization in each case depends on how a judge views the particular facts, the same kind of chattel may be a fixture in some settings and not in others. As Bruce Ziff observes, the "structurally equivocal dwelling known as a 'mobile home' illustrates this indeterminacy, since the case law on whether mobile homes are fixtures divides into two camps. None of the mobile home rulings is necessarily wrong; so much depends on the facts." (*Principles of Property Law*, 3rd ed., (Scarborough, ON: Carswell, 2000) at 106).

As in any situation where legal rights rest on sometimes obscure legal distinctions, parties can use contracts to ensure that the legal consequences of a transaction will match their expectations. If, on the facts, something is a fixture, a contract cannot make it into a chattel by calling it a chattel. But the parties to a contract for the sale of real estate can, for example, write into their agreement of purchase and sale that the vendor will remove the crystal chandelier in the dining room and repair any damage before completion of the sale, or that the purchase includes the mirror over the mantle, the wall-to-wall carpeting, and the dock and changing shed that are hauled up to the boat house for winter storage.

## CROPS AND TREES

Crops, although they too are attached to the land, are not considered fixtures because their attachment to the land is intended to be temporary. Emblements is the legal term for growing crops annually produced by the labour of the cultivator. Even before harvest, while the crops are still attached to the land — and indeed, even before they are planted — the landowner can transfer rights to the crop without transferring rights to the land itself. Thus, the landowner can obtain a loan for planting a crop and give the creditor an interest in the crop as security for the loan. In general, a growing crop is treated as a chattel and not part of the real property, but a transfer of land transfers rights to any standing crop on the land, unless the owner of the land no longer owns the crop, or unless the crop is specifically excluded from the property being transferred.

Trees are neither emblements nor fixtures. They remain rooted to the land for much longer than emblements, and are generally treated as part of the land in a transfer of a freehold estate. In England, where most of our common law rules originated, individual trees as well as a managed forest could be a significant part of the value of the estate, and a person who holds a life estate is constrained by the doctrine of waste, discussed in Chapter Two, from harvesting trees beyond what is necessary to meet reasonable needs for fuel and shelter. In the colonies, where the first objective of many settlers was clearing the land in order to plant crops, judges were willing to reconceptualize how much tree-cutting would maintain a reasonable balance between the competing ownership rights of the life tenant and the person entitled to possession of the fee simple when the life tenant died.

Not uncommonly, people plant trees to mark the boundary lines of their property, and, as these grow and spread, their presence may occasion disputes over who has the right to cut them. If the trunk of the tree emerges from the ground entirely on A's property, A has the right to cut the tree, but not to trespass on a neighbour's land to do so. B, the neighbour, has the right to cut the branches that overhang on B's property. Some decisions suggest further that B has the right to cut away any part of a tree trunk that is on B's land, without A's permission and without liability to A if the tree dies. Prudent people, however, obtain agreement from their neighbours before interfering with a tree whose ownership is not entirely clear. Why risk being the defendant in the case that clarifies the law to the benefit of the plaintiff?

## REGISTRATION OF INTERESTS IN LAND

At common law, the right to a legal freehold estate in land was transferred in a ceremony called feoffment by livery of seisin, described in Chapter Two. This ceremony, held on the land itself, gave notice to the community of who claimed rights in the land and who had the obligations of landholding. Equitable estates, as will be discussed in Chapter Nine, could be transferred without these physical ceremonies, and so the transfers could be effected in secret. In 1535, the English Parliament, at the instigation of the King, Henry VIII, tried to prevent secret transfers with passage of the *Statute of Enrolments, 1535* (U.K.), 27 Hen. 8, c. 16, requiring registration of the commonest form of transfers of title to estates in land. Clever conveyancers, however, quickly developed new forms of transfers to avoid this requirement, and most conveyances of estates in land continued to be recorded only in documents held by the family solicitor, not deposited in any public registry.

Newly established colonial legislatures usually provided for transfer of estates in land by deed, and public registration of land transfers. Transfers of estates in land by deed were effected by signing, sealing and delivering the deed to the purchaser; registration was not generally necessary to validate the transfer. Registration, however, had two significant advantages. Registration of the deed or other instrument by which one acquired an interest in the land gave notice to the world of one's interest in the land, and a registered interest, with some exceptions, took priority over an unregistered interest.

### Registry Systems

Ontario and the four Atlantic provinces early in their history established Registries of Deeds, for recording and indexing deeds and other instruments creating interests in land. The registry provides a public repository of documents, with the date of their recording carefully noted. In a registry system, the registrar does not make any assessment of whether the documents in the registry office are valid to create the interests in land they claim to create. That is the responsibility of those who use the documents to establish a chain of title.

The Atlantic provinces indexed the documents in their registry offices by the names of the grantors and grantees, an approach consistent with some older descriptions of parcels of land that identify the parcel by identifying the owners of all of the neighbouring parcels. In Ontario, where much of the land was surveyed before the Crown issued the first Crown grants, the records were usually indexed by lot number, according to the location of the parcel on a survey grid.

### Land Titles or Torrens Systems

The Canadian colonies established to the west of Ontario implemented the Land Titles or Torrens system, developed by Sir Robert Torrens and first implemented in the colony of South Australia in 1858. In the Torrens system, the government not only provides a public office for recording interests in land, but investigates the claims made in those documents and guarantees their validity.

Ontario has for many years maintained a land titles registration system alongside an active registry system; beginning in 1999, with the introduction of electronic registration of land-related documents, the province began converting land records from the registry system to the land titles system. Nova Scotia and New Brunswick are also currently converting to a land titles system. Without legislation making registration and conversion compulsory, it may be a long process, as individual owners are reluctant to pay for the extensive title search necessary to prepare a registry title for first registration in a land titles system.

## ACQUIRING INTERESTS BY ADVERSE POSSESSION

At common law, as discussed in Chapter Two, the person who is seised of a freehold estate in land is the person entitled to legal possession of the land. In ordinary parlance, we would call that person the owner, or the title holder. Registration of title gives notice to the world of the title holder's claim to the land. But if someone other than the title holder has actual physical possession of the land, without the title holder's permission, then that person's presence on the land is an assertion to the world of another claim to hold the rights of an owner.

Under the doctrine of adverse possession, the title holder has a limited time period to dispute the assertion of ownership based on possession, through taking legal action to remove the person in possession. That time period is specified in the applicable statute of limitations, and in the Canadian provinces and territories, it is generally 10 or 20 years, with a longer limitation period, up to 60 years, if the title holder is the Crown. If the title holder fails to take action against the adverse possessor within the statutory time limit, then the title holder loses the right to take any action, and the adverse possessor acquires the rights of ownership.

In effect, the doctrine of adverse possession requires title holders to "use it or lose it", at least in contexts in which someone else is using the land. Most commonly, though, the doctrine is invoked not to give a squatter title, but to settle title problems, where the legal description of a particular parcel of land does not match the physical boundaries maintained between two neighbours. Indeed, the doctrine is defended as helping ensure certainty of title and therefore lower transaction costs on land transfers.

To establish rights by adverse possession, the non-title holder has to prove sufficient possession of the land for a sufficient time period. The latter is determined by the relevant statute of limitations, but the former is determined by looking at the quality of the possession that is reasonable given the nature of the land claimed. Possession must be adverse, that is, without the permission, and to the exclusion, of the title holder, and sufficiently open and notorious that it will (or should) be obvious to all. Possession must be actual physical occupation — what some judges call *pedis possessio* or pedal possession — evidenced by physical alterations to the land, showing the adverse possessor's control over the land. Thus, it is much more difficult to acquire rights by adverse possession to large tracts of undeveloped land than to the two-foot strip along the side of your suburban lot that you have been using as part of your driveway.

There is one exception to the requirement for actual physical possession. Adverse possessors who establish actual physical occupation of part of a parcel of land, in the mistaken, but reasonably-held, belief that they have the right to legal possession, are said to have colour of title. Just as title holders have constructive possession without physical possession of the whole of what they own, so adverse possessors in possession of part of a parcel of land under colour of title have constructive possession of the whole. Constructive possession, of course, is defeated by proof of actual possession — otherwise, there would be no doctrine of adverse possession.

Most land titles systems prohibit claims based on adverse possession, in order to maintain the completeness and accuracy of the title record in the land titles office. When a government decides to convert its land registry to a land titles system, it usually imposes quite stringent requirements for proving the validity of the interests in land claimed in documents presented for first registration in the land titles system. Often, the person applying for first registration will have to resort to the doctrine of adverse possession to establish precise boundaries; once the title documents are accepted for registration in the land titles system, however, further claims based on adverse possession are barred.

## LAND USE REGULATION

The owner of a fee simple estate owns the most comprehensive bundle of rights in land that a person can own at common law or in equity, but the rights of the fee simple owner are not without limit. Zoning by-laws may limit what owners can do with their land through prohibiting some uses entirely, and segregating other uses, such as residential, industrial or commercial, into different geographic areas. Zoning by-laws can also segregate neighbourhoods by income level, by specifying that lots must be a minimum size and structures on them of a minimum value. Private covenants, as discussed in Chapter Seven, may do the same thing.

Most Canadian jurisdictions also have a variety of statutes protecting distinctive environments or the habitats of rare or endangered species. Regulations made pursuant to these statutes may prohibit the landowner from stripping topsoil, draining wetlands, or even building on the property. Such regulation does not give landowners the right to claim compensation for expropriation, even though they may be unable to use their land as they wish, unless the regulation eliminates "virtually all of the aggregated incidents of ownership . . . having regard to the nature of the land and the range of reasonable uses to which it has actually been put": *Mariner Real Estate Ltd. v. Nova Scotia (Attorney General)*, [1999] N.S.J. No. 283 at para. 49, 178 N.S.R. (2d) 294 (N.S.C.A.).

Some provinces also regulate access to land ownership, to achieve specific land use goals. Prince Edward Island sets an absolute ownership limit of 1,000 acres for individuals and 3,000 acres for corporations, with lower limits for non-residents wishing to acquire land on the coast. Some jurisdictions limit total ownership and non-resident ownership of agricultural land, and prohibit conversion of agricultural land to non-agricultural uses.

To facilitate private initiatives to preserve land from development and to protect species habitat and fragile or unique ecosystems, some provinces have created a new statutory form of property interest variously called conservation easements, covenants or servitudes. Generally, to create a conservation easement, a landowner signs an agreement with a government or non-governmental organization defining the permitted uses of a defined parcel of land. Once the agreement is registered in the appropriate registry or land titles office, it is enforceable by the other party to the agreement, and binds future purchasers of the land. The names used for these property interests suggest an analogy with the real property interests discussed in Chapter Seven, but those interests can be created only to benefit neighbouring land, not other living organisms.

# 6

# FIRST NATIONS RIGHTS TO LAND AND NATURAL RESOURCES

So far, we have been looking at land law as it developed in England, to help us understand land ownership in modern common law jurisdictions. In Chapter One, we noted that English law was brought to the lands that we now call Canada with the first British settlers. But North America was already occupied by aboriginal peoples with their own political organizations, custom and laws. In this chapter, we consider the contemporary basis of aboriginal peoples' rights to land and natural resources.

First Nations peoples in Canada have rights based on their continuing use and occupation of their traditional territory after French and British colonizers asserted their claims to sovereignty in what they referred to as "the new world". These rights continue despite the assertion of European sovereignty until they are extinguished by the colonizing power, or relinquished in a treaty between the colonizing power and the First Nations collectivity that holds the rights. With the affirmation of these rights in s. 35 of the *Constitution Act, 1982*, being Schedule B to the *Canada Act 1982* (U.K.), c. 11, the government can no longer extinguish them unilaterally.

## THE "NUMBERED" TREATIES AND THEIR PRE-CONFEDERATION ANTECEDENTS

In the 19th and early 20th century, British and then Canadian policymakers entered into treaties with aboriginal peoples to clear them from land that the government wanted for European settlers. Between 1871 and 1921, the federal government negotiated 11 treaties, called the "numbered treaties", with the aboriginal peoples occupying land in what is now northwestern Ontario, the prairie provinces, northeastern British Columbia and parts of Yukon, the Northwest Territories and Nunavut.

The numbered treaties were modelled on the earlier Robinson Treaties (1850) in what is now Ontario, and the Douglas Treaties (1850-1859) on what is now Vancouver Island. In these treaties, First Nations collectivities surrendered their rights to their land, in return for promises of reserve lands and provision of education and health care. Many of the treaties also recognized the right of First Nations peoples to continue to hunt, fish and gather on unoccupied land. The recognition and meaning of these treaties in the 21st century remains a matter of negotiation and, sometimes, litigation. The federal government has established a specific claims policy to deal with unresolved issues, such as allocation of reserves lands, under the historic treaties.

## THE COMPREHENSIVE LAND CLAIMS POLICY AND MODERN TREATY-MAKING

The Supreme Court of Canada decision in *Calder v. British Columbia (Attorney General)*, [1973] S.C.J. No. 56, [1973] S.C.R. 313 (S.C.C.) changed existing thinking on aboriginal rights and opened the way for the modern land claims process. In *Calder*, the Nisga'a sought a declaration that they owned their traditional lands in the Nass Valley in what is now British Columbia. Of the seven judges who participated in the decision at the Supreme Court, six ruled that the Nisga'a had aboriginal title at the time that the British acquired sovereignty over the area of the claim. Three of the judges ruled as well that the Nisga'a title still existed; three ruled that it had been extinguished. The seventh judge, Justice Pigeon, dismissed the Nisga'a claim on the basis of a procedural defect in bringing the case to court. The Nisga'a thus failed to obtain recognition of their aboriginal title, but they considered the decision a victory nonetheless, because it affirmed the possibility of a continuing aboriginal right to lands they had traditionally occupied.

Following the *Calder* decision, the federal government implemented a comprehensive land claims policy to settle outstanding First Nations lands claims. As of 2011, the federal and provincial or territorial governments had signed comprehensive land claims settlement treaties covering parts of British Columbia, Northern Québec, Labrador, Yukon and the Northwest Territories. These included a treaty with the Nisga'a, which came into effect in 2000, and a treaty providing for creation of the new territory of Nunavut in 1999. In the comprehensive land claims agreements, First Nations collectivities relinquish their claim to aboriginal title over their extensive traditional lands in exchange for recognized and enforceable rights over a more limited area. Even though the federal government has the constitutional responsibility for First Nations matters, the provincial governments participate in treaty negotiations because it is the Crown in right of the province that owns public lands in the province, and that will benefit from having the lands freed of the claim to aboriginal title.

The Alberta government, acting independently of the federal government, negotiated a settlement with Métis peoples providing a secure land base, development funds and some self-government for Métis living in eight settlement areas in northern Alberta. Tri-partite negotiations continue across the country, including in Atlantic Canada, both to resolve outstanding land claims and to establish the terms on which First Nations will resume their right of self-government.

## THE TREATIES OF PEACE AND FRIENDSHIP IN ATLANTIC CANADA: *R. V. MARSHALL*

In September 1999, the Supreme Court of Canada released its decision in *R. v. Marshall*, [1999] S.C.J. No. 55, [1999] 3 S.C.R. 456 (S.C.C.), motion for rehearing and stay dismissed [1999] S.C.J. No. 66, [1999] 3 S.C.R. 533 (S.C.C.), allowing Donald Marshall's appeal against his conviction on charges of catching and selling eels in violation of federal fisheries regulations. Marshall, a Mi'kmaq from Nova Scotia, asserted that, under treaties signed in 1760-61, Mi'kmaq people had the right to fish and to sell fish without having to comply with federal regulations. The Court, in a five-to-two decision, agreed, basing its ruling on the "truckhouse clause" of the Mi'kmac Treaties of 1760-61, which reads as follows (para. 5):

> And I do further promise for myself and my tribe that we will not either directly nor indirectly assist any of the enemies of His most sacred Majesty King George the Second, his heirs or Successors, nor hold any manner of Commerce traffick nor intercourse with them, but on the contrary will as much as may be in our power discover and make known to His Majesty's Governor, any ill designs which may be formed or contrived against His Majesty's subjects. And I do further engage that we will not traffick, barter or Exchange any Commodities in any manner but with such persons or the managers of such Truck houses as shall be appointed or Established by His Majesty's Governor at Lunenbourg or Elsewhere in Nova Scotia or Acadia.

The majority held that this clause, when read in light of the British need for peace with the Mi'kmaq during a period of war with France, implicitly recognized the right to hunt and fish to obtain goods to trade. The Court ruled, however, that the right to trade was limited to trade to obtain necessaries, defined for the modern context as a right to secure "a moderate livelihood", or "food, clothing and housing, supplemented by a few amenities"; that is, something beyond "bare subsistence" but not enough for the "accumulation of wealth".

It follows that hunting and fishing rights recognized in the 1760-61 Treaties are limited by the definition of a moderate livelihood. They are also limited by the right of the government, as determined by earlier Supreme Court decisions on aboriginal hunting and fishing rights, to enforce hunting and fishing regulations intended to protect the stock or for some other purpose of public importance, such as public safety or general economic development. The government has the onus of demonstrating that such regulations are necessary for the stated purpose, and that they infringe as little as possible on the rights of First Nations people. Such justification is more difficult if the regulations have been put in place without any consultation with First Nations peoples.

## THE REQUIREMENTS FOR PROVING ABORIGINAL TITLE

Despite three centuries of treaty-making, much of Canada remains subject to aboriginal claims to land and resources. Cases concerning the extent of the aboriginal rights recognized and affirmed in s. 35 of the *Constitution Act, 1982* come to court in various ways. In *Calder* and in *Delgamuukw v. British Columbia*, [1997] S.C.J. No. 108, [1997] 3 S.C.R. 1010 (S.C.C.), the First Nations collectivities were plaintiffs, seeking a declaration recognizing their claims to aboriginal title. More often, as with the treaty rights at issue in *Marshall*, First Nations individuals are defendants in a criminal or quasi-criminal proceeding in which they are charged with hunting, fishing or cutting wood without complying with federal, provincial or territorial regulations. That was the situation in *R. v. Marshall; R v. Bernard*, [2005] S.C.J. No. 44, [2005] 2 S.C.R. 220 (S.C.C.), discussed below. In appeals from Nova Scotia and New Brunswick respectively, the defendants relied on their claims to aboriginal title to justify their harvesting of wood from Crown land without having first obtained a licence from the Crown.

Whether relying on aboriginal or treaty rights, the person or collectivity claiming the right has the responsibility of establishing the necessary factual basis for the right. Consequently, these cases may involve weeks of expert testimony from historians, anthropologists, and other social scientists, as well as evidence from aboriginal elders regarding the collectivity's traditional use of the land. In *Delgamuukw*, the Supreme Court overturned the trial judge's rejection of the aboriginal claim, because the judge had failed to give sufficient weight to the oral history presented by the aboriginal elders. Because this failure may have led to erroneous findings on the factual question of whether the plaintiffs had occupied the land claimed in the way necessary to establish a claim to ownership or aboriginal title, the Supreme Court ordered a new trial, while expressing its hope that the parties would reach a negotiated solution.

To provide guidance for future negotiations and litigation, the Supreme Court in *Delgamuukw* reviewed the basic principles of aboriginal title. The court described aboriginal title as an aboriginal right that is more than the right to engage in specific activities, such as hunting, fishing, or gathering for sustenance, ceremonial or trading purposes. Aboriginal title, unlike other aboriginal rights, includes the right to exclusive use and occupation of the land, subject only to the limitation that the uses must not be irreconcilable with the nature of the aboriginal attachment to the land that forms the basis of the aboriginal title.

Aboriginal title thus shares some of the features of ownership of a fee simple estate in land, but it is *sui generis*, meaning in a class by itself, distinct from the fee simple estate. Aboriginal title arises from exclusive occupation of land by a First Nations collectivity at the time that Europeans acquired sovereignty over the area. Because the title belongs to the collectivity as a whole, lands held in aboriginal title cannot be transferred, sold, or surrendered to First Nations individuals or non-aboriginals; the lands can be transferred only to the Crown.

Present occupation of the land can be evidence of occupation pre-sovereignty, if the claimants prove continuity between present and past occupation. This continuity need not be unbroken, as that requirement would deny aboriginal title to collectivities whose use and occupation of an area was disrupted by European incursions. Where aboriginal collectivities can establish use or occupancy but not the exclusivity necessary for aboriginal title, the collectivity may be able to establish other aboriginal rights, such as the right to hunt and fish in a specific area, or to have access to specific sites for ceremonial purposes.

European acquisition of sovereignty is the relevant date for establishing the occupation necessary to prove aboriginal title, rather than the time of first contact between Europeans and the First Nations people, because the concept of aboriginal title becomes necessary only when there are other claims to title. As well, because aboriginal title is a general right of use and occupation of land rather than its use for specific purposes distinctive to aboriginal society, there is no need to distinguish traditional uses from those that are the consequence of European contact.

These criteria for establishing aboriginal title were clarified in *Marshall* and *Bernard*. Chief Justice McLachlin, writing for the majority, focused on three specific requirements for proving aboriginal title: continuity of connection with the pre-sovereignty group upon whose occupation of the land the claimants base their claim to title; exclusive occupation; and physical occupation.

In *Delgamuukw*, Chief Justice Lamer held that the aboriginal collectivity asserting a claim to title could overcome a lack of evidence as to occupation at the date of sovereignty by extrapolating backwards from current occupancy, providing they could establish some continuity between present and pre-sovereignty occupation. Chief Justice McLachlin's discussion of the continuity requirement in *Marshall and Bernard* seems to elevate it from an alternative means of proving pre-sovereignty occupation to an independent requirement for proving aboriginal title.

Chief Justice McLachlin also raised the standard of proof of exclusive occupation, requiring that aboriginal claimants demonstrate that their ancestors intended to, and did, exclude others from their traditional territory. She rejected the conclusion of Justice Daigle in the New Brunwick Court of Appeal that peaceable relations between various aboriginal groups, in which each respected the territorial claims of of the other, was sufficient to establish proof of exclusive occupation, without need for "evidence of the negative side, of forced exclusion of others, or of hostile acts or violence where none exists": *R. v. Bernard*, [2003] N.B.J. No. 320 at para. 148, 230 D.L.R. (4th) 57 (N.B.C.A.). As well, Justice Daigle noted that the Mi'kmaq undertaking in the Peace and Friendship Treaties of 1760 and 1761 to live amicably with the British was "a manifestation of their fundamental cultural attribute as a hospitable and sharing people" (at para. 165). He rejected the Crown's attempt to use that agreement to attack the Mi'kmaq claim to aboriginal title, characterizing it as inconsistent with the honour and good faith of the Crown (at paras. 166-167).

On the issue of physical occupation, Chief Justice McLachlin seemed to require the same kind of proof of physical occupation that is required to prove rights to land by adverse possession at common law. The evidence established that the timber harvesting site in *Bernard* was within the area traditionally occupied seasonally by the Mi'kmaq, but the Chief Justice characterized this evidence as showing only "irregular use of undefined lands", when what was required was proof of "regular use of defined lands".

As we saw in Chapter Five, at common law, if a person claims title to land by adverse possession, the claimant has to show actual physical possession of the land sufficient to displace the constructive possession enjoyed by the holder of the title to land. Generally, physical possession is established with evidence of activity that visibly and substantially changes the land, such as felling trees to make fields or pastures, cultivating the land, and erecting fences and buildings. Many First Nations communities sustained themselves from the land in ways that did not leave this kind of physical evidence of their occupation.

In *Delgamuukw*, the court used terms such as "physical presence", "presence amounting to occupancy" or "use and occupation" rather than the term "possession", in order to maintain a distinction between the quality of possession required to establish aboriginal title and the quality required to establish rights by adverse possession. Justice LeBel, writing for himself and Justice Fish in the Supreme Court decision in *Marshall* and *Bernard*, recognized that conflating aboriginal title with common law title could deny any aboriginal rights in traditional lands, because aboriginal views of property or land use did not fit within what Justice LeBel referred to as "Euro-centric conceptions of property rights". Nonetheless, the Supreme Court in *Marshall* and *Bernard* rejected the claim of aboriginal title, and the accused were found guilty of illegally harvesting timber on Crown land. Given the nature of the evidence required to establish aboriginal rights or treaty rights, however, the decision was not a final determination of the question of aboriginal title.

Aboriginal law is a growing field, as more cases work their way up through the courts to the Supreme Court, and as more First Nations acquire recognition of their rights to land, natural resources, and self-government. Whatever the ruling in individual cases, First Nations across Canada are no longer willing to watch while others profit from resources that once were theirs.

Canadian courts have required that governments must consult with aboriginal peoples before undertaking or authorizing activity that has the potential to infringe on existing aboriginal or treaty rights, even if these rights have not yet been confirmed in a judicial ruling. The Crown's duty to consult does not give First Nations a veto over development, but in an appropriate consultation, the Crown will give affected First Nations collectivities timely notice of the proposed activity, listen respectfully to their concerns, consider how to minimize the impact of the activity on aboriginal or treaty rights, and provide compensation for the infringement. Failure to conduct an appropriate consultation can delay or derail a proposed activity. Until aboriginal people have received justice, others' access to Crown land and resources rests on a shaky foundation.

# 7

# LICENCES, INCORPOREAL HEREDITAMENTS AND COVENANTS

This chapter deals with some of the interests in land that are less than estates, and might thus be subtitled, "rights in the land of another". We have seen that the holder of a fee simple or other estate in land can transfer all or part of the circle of rights and obligations that makes up ownership of the estate in order to create an estate — freehold or leasehold — in the transferee. The kind of estate that is transferred defines the duration of the rights of the transferee, and determines what estate, if any, the transferor retains.

All grants of estates are grants of an extensive bundle of rights and obligations. Included in these bundles are some rights that can be transferred without changing the kind of estate that O retains. These rights are qualitatively and quantitatively less than those forming estates; their transfer diminishes O's rights without creating an estate in the transferee. These rights may be divided into three main categories: licences; *profits à prendre* and easements (these two together are known as "incorporeal hereditaments"); and covenants. Each is quite distinct conceptually, with different rules for creation and continuation, but performs similar functions. As we examine each in turn, consider which will best meet the needs of particular situations.

## LICENCES

Licences fit awkwardly with land law because they are mere personal rights, not interests in land. The holder of a licence may, however, have rights with respect to use of land, and in some circumstances these rights may develop into an interest in land, as we will see. Consider what happens when the operator of a parking lot permits the owner of a car, for a fee, to leave the car on the parking lot. The parking lot operator has granted the car owner a licence to use the parking lot. Of course, leaving the car may also create a bailment relationship, if the car owner transfers possession of the car to the parking lot operator. But bailment in this situation defines the relationship with respect to the car. Licence defines the relationship with respect to the land.

A licence is permission to do something with respect to land, that, without the permission, would be a trespass. The permission may be granted orally or in writing; it may be given expressly or by implication — as in the licence extended to the public to enter a store when it is open for business. Generally, licences are not transferable. A licence that is given gratuitously, called a "bare licence", is almost always revocable at the will of the grantor; revocation of licences given for consideration, such as the permission, for a fee, to leave one's car on a parking lot, will be governed by the contractual terms defining the licence.

There is some support in modern case law for blurring the distinction between personal and proprietary rights. In some circumstances, judges have held that rights given by contract or licence have become like proprietary rights by the working of an estoppel. In effect, with a licence, the landowner may be estopped from revoking the licence. Where the licence holder, acting on reasonable expectations created by the words or conduct of the landowner, has contributed money or labour to the improvement of the landowner's property, the landowner may be prevented from appropriating the improvements. The remedy may be compensation to the licence holder, if the licence is revoked, or an order that the licence be made irrevocable. In some cases, judges have converted rights granted under licence into an interest or estate in land. An alternative remedy in situations of unjust enrichment would be an order that the landowner holds title to the property on a constructive trust for the benefit of the person who made the contribution, as discussed in Chapter Nine.

## INCORPOREAL HEREDITAMENTS

A hereditament is a property right that is capable of being inherited; incorporeal here means intangible. Hence, an incorporeal hereditament is an intangible property right that can be transferred. It does not give one the right to possess another's land, but the right to make some use or to restrain certain uses of another's land. There are two categories of incorporeal hereditaments: *profits à prendre* and easements. Both developed as interests in land when contract doctrine was relatively undeveloped. Today, rights that were once granted as incorporeal hereditaments might be secured more effectively by contract. Personal rights secured by contract, however, are not proprietary rights, and might not bind successors in title.

### *Profits à prendre*

A *profit à prendre* is the right to enter the land of another to harvest specific natural produce of the land, such as timber, crops, minerals, turf, peat, sand, soil, fish or animals. The thing taken must be part of the land — minerals or crops, for example — or wild animals existing on the land.

Rights to take water may be granted as easements but not as *profits à prendre*.

The profit is somewhat like a licence in that it can exist in gross; that is, one can have a profit even if one owns no land nearby that will benefit from the profit. For example, an owner of a profit of piscary, discussed in Chapter Five, can transfer the profit of piscary to a non-riparian owner, as an exclusive or non-exclusive right. Unlike the licence, the profit is a real property right. The grantor can not revoke it unilaterally, and it is transferable, as an exclusive or non-exclusive right.

In the oil and gas industry, the right to enter another's land to extract subterranean oil and gas is often granted in an instrument referred to as an oil and gas lease. In *Berkheiser v. Berkheiser*, [1957] S.C.J. No. 22, [1957] S.C.R. 387 (S.C.C.), the Supreme Court of Canada held that an oil and gas lease generally creates a *profit à prendre*. Holders of a *profit à prendre* under an oil and gas lease do not own the oil or gas in the ground — *in situ*, as the cases say — but will obtain title to the oil and gas when they have taken possession of it by bringing it to the surface. The *profit à prendre* created by an oil and gas lease includes rights that are possessory in nature, permitting the leaseholder to bring actions of trespass at common law for actions that interfere with the right to recover the substances granted in the lease.

In most circumstances, a leasehold estate granted for an indefinite period would be void for uncertainty, but the grant of a *profit à prendre* in oil and gas leases may be for an indefinite period of time. Oil and gas leases are often structured with a primary term, expressed as a term of years, and, if oil and gas is produced during the primary term, a secondary term that may continue as long as the leaseholder continues to produce the leased substances.

## Easements

An easement is a non-possessory interest in the land of another. The most commonly known form of easement is a right of way, giving a landowner access across a neighbour's land. Many varied rights can exist as easements. Although judges are cautious about granting property status to new claims, the list of possible easements is not completely closed. One can acquire by easement the right to prevent a neighbour from erecting structures that would interfere with the air and light to one's window, or to compel a neighbour to provide support for a semi-detached house. An easement is sometimes a grant of permission to do what would otherwise be actionable in tort as a nuisance or a trespass, as with an easement to drain water across a neighbour's land or to have one's roof extend over a neighbour's lot.

In each of these examples, there is a relationship between neighbours, as well as a right in another's land that is connected to the uses one makes of one's own land. In technical legal language, we say that a right is not an easement unless there is a dominant and a servient tenement, that is, a property that enjoys the easement and a property that supplies it. Easements cannot exist in gross — you cannot own an easement unless you own land that benefits from the easement. You may have a licence to take a shortcut across a property that lies between the street where you park and the office where you work, but such a right cannot be an easement if you do not own either the office or the parking spot. The requirement for owning land to be benefitted is one of the distinctions, in the Canadian common law jurisdictions, between a *profit à prendre* and an easement; in some American jurisdictions, though, easements may exist in gross. As we saw in Chapter Five, the new conservation easement may exist in gross. And municipalities, public utility companies and similar entities may have statutory easements giving them access to private property as necessary to carry out their operations, without the requirement for owning neighbouring property.

Because the easement must be a right that one property-holder grants to another, it follows that the dominant and servient tenements must be owned and occupied by different people — it is not possible to grant an easement to oneself. Although this point may seem trivial now, we will return to it when we talk about how easements are created and extinguished.

We have described the holders of the dominant and the servient tenements as neighbours. How close must the properties be to each other? They need not adjoin, but they must be close enough so that the easement can serve the dominant tenement. To be an easement, the right must benefit the land itself, not just add to the convenience, pleasure, or profit of the person who owns or occupies the land at the time. The essence of the difference is that an easement is a right in and for land, not a right of an individual.

So far, then, we have stated three of the four requirements for an easement: a dominant and a servient tenement; a right that benefits the dominant tenement; and separate owners and occupiers of the dominant and servient tenements. The fourth requirement is that the right in question must be one that is capable of forming the subject matter of a grant. It must be a property right, limited in scope, defined clearly, and described adequately.

### *Acquiring easements*

The ordinary way of creating any property right is by grant, *inter vivos* or testamentary. Easements can be created by grant or reservation from a grant, either express or implied. In the absence of a grant, easements can be acquired by prescription through proof of long use. Even here, the legal theory presumes that the long use is pursuant to a grant that was lost. In most jurisdictions, statutes of limitations or easement Acts set out the requirements for acquiring an easement by prescription, but one may still be able to plead a lost modern grant. Under either claim, the claimant must show that the long use — usually for 20 years — was *nec vi, nec clam*, and *nec precario*, that is, use without violence or any coercive means, not clandestinely but openly, and as of right rather than by permission. It is not easy to acquire an easement by prescription, for, as the Ontario Court of Appeal said in *Temma Realty Co. v. Ress Enterprises Ltd.*, [1968] O.J. No. 1152 at para. 9, [1968] 2 O.R. 293 (Ont. C.A.), the court tends to prevent "neighbourly accommodation from ripening into a legal right".

The clearest and simplest way to create an easement is for O, the owner of the servient tenement, to execute a deed (draw up, sign, and deliver an instrument under seal) to A granting A rights to make use of O's land or to restrict O's use of the land in specified ways for specified purposes. Since O has the servient tenement, O will want to define the easement as narrowly as possible. It is also possible for O to grant a freehold estate to A, but to retain, by a reservation in the grant, the right to an easement over the property that is being transferred. Hence, if O decides to subdivide property and sell part to A, O may reserve to the benefit of the part retained a right of way over the part to be sold. In the deed from O to A, O conveys the property to A and reserves the easement, identifying the land sold to A as the servient tenement and the land retained as the dominant tenement.

Suppose that the property being divided is bordered on one side by the main road and on the opposite side by a lovely lake, with a laneway that goes from the road to the lake. O wants to keep the lakefront but sell off the part along the road. While O owns the entire property, it does not make sense to talk of O's use of the laneway between road and lake as an easement, since O cannot have an easement over land that it owns and occupies. But we can think of O's use of the laneway as a quasi-easement. When O sells the roadside lot, O will want to keep a right of way to the road, and O may want to give the roadside lot access to the lake, to get a higher price. In this case, O would execute a deed granting the roadside lot to A, with a right of way along the laneway for access to the lake. In the same deed, O would reserve a right of way along A's part of the laneway, to give the lakefront lot access to the road.

But what if, in the example just given, somebody errs and one or both of the easements is omitted from the deed? It may then be possible to assert a right to an easement by implied grant or reservation from grant. Will it make any difference whether it is O claiming an easement by implied reservation or A by implied grant? Most definitely. It is almost impossible for grantors to acquire an easement by implied reservation, because that would be derogating from their grant. In other words, although by deed O expressly conveyed all the rights in the fee simple to A, O now wants some of those rights back in the form of an easement. If O wanted those rights, O should have reserved them from the grant. But where O has sold property to A and the easement is necessary for A's intended use of the property, to refuse to hold that O has granted, by implication, the easement along with the fee simple would again allow O to derogate from the grant. Thus the courts will imply a grant of an easement from O to A if A needs it for access to the land, or to make effective use of the estate granted. These are the same circumstances in which a court will imply a reservation of an easement. But for O to acquire rights by an implied reservation, O will have to prove that the easement is strictly necessary for the use of the property, not just that it will make the use more convenient.

In addition, a grantee may be able to acquire an easement by implied grant by proving three things: (1) that at the time of the grant, the right now claimed as an easement was being exercised by the owner of the property for the benefit of the property; (2) that the use is necessary for the reasonable enjoyment of the property; and (3) that this use continues and is apparent from physical evidence on the property. In this way, a grantee might be able to claim an easement for use of an existing laneway across the grantor's land or even for passage of sewer pipes if their existence is shown by a band of greener grass across the grantor's property.

Note that there cannot be an implied grant or reservation of an easement if the parties do not stand in the relationship of grantor and grantee. That is, if you buy land-locked property from someone who retains no land around it, you may be able to negotiate a right of way from your neighbours but you have no right to one. Planning legislation relating to subdivisions and statutory provisions stating that grants of the fee simple include grants of what pertains to the property — houses, trees, easements, *etc.* — may save you from such a dilemma, but the common law rule is "buyer, beware; an ounce of prevention is worth a pound of cure".

### *Scope of easements*

Changes in use of the dominant tenement may increase the burden on the servient tenement through changes in the use of the easement. For example, when O granted a right of way to A along its laneway to reach A's seaside retreat, A may have had nothing on the property but a beached boat. What if A now has a hotel, restaurant and golf course? Can A's guests use the laneway? If A subdivides the dominant estate into 50 lots, can each of the 50 grantees now use the laneway? These are questions about the scope of the easement.

The description of the easement in the grant, if it is well-drafted, should provide the answer. Alas, even experienced practitioners cannot anticipate all potential issues in advance, and so courts look to the purpose for which the easement was granted in determining whether a change in use comes within the scope of the original grant. An easement given for passage by horse and wagon, then, would likely be construed today as permitting passage of automobiles. The test is whether allowing the new use will amount to the imposition of an increased burden on the servient tenement so as to materially alter the position of that land and its owner.

If the original easement was created by implication in a grant subdividing a parcel of land, rather than by express grant, the permitted scope of use will be determined by the manner in which the quasi-easement was used when the parcel had a single owner. With easements acquired by prescription, the purpose and scope is established by evidence of what rights were exercised during the prescription period. Existing use then becomes the standard for determining the permissible uses.

### *Extinguishing easements*

Easements, being created by grant, can be extinguished in the same way — by the owner of the dominant tenement executing a deed releasing the servient tenement from the burden of the easement. Easements can also be extinguished by implication if the easement no longer benefits the dominant tenement. Mere non-use will not extinguish an easement; there must be evidence of an intention to abandon the easement, shown, for example, by a change in the use of the dominant tenement that makes the easement useless. In some jurisdictions, land registration statutes may extinguish easements that are not registered on title if the servient tenement is acquired by a *bona fide* purchaser for value without notice of the easement.

Since one of the requirements for an easement is that the dominant and servient tenements are owned and occupied by different people, existing easements will be extinguished if one person acquires both tenements. When one person acquires the fee simple to one tenement and possession of the other, the easement is not extinguished but only suspended. This would occur, for example, when the owner of the fee simple in the dominant tenement acquires the servient tenement for a one-year lease. The easement will be suspended for that year but will revive when possession reverts to the landlord.

Finally, easements which are inherently connected with structures rather than with the land itself are open to a rather unique form of destruction. If one has a right of way over a staircase in house A as a means of access to house B, and house A is destroyed, does the easement disappear? There is not much doubt that if house A, the servient tenement, is destroyed by what are called acts of God — a tempest, flood or earthquake — then there is no obligation to rebuild the staircase for the benefit of B. Authority is divided on whether A may tear down the house to make an alternate use of the land, incidentally destroying the easement. Even though, in general, the owner of the servient tenement is not required to spend money to maintain the easement, the tendency of the cases is to prevent A from destroying the house and the accompanying easement without the consent of B, the owner of the dominant tenement.

### *Public "easements"*

Since easements must benefit a nearby property, a person who does not own rights in nearby land cannot acquire an easement over another's land, because such a right would be a personal benefit, not a right attaching to land. We have noted already the possibility of statutory easements in favour of public bodies. What about public rights of way? If, over the course of many years, members of the public cross O's land and create a path over it (without complaint from O), O may eventually lose the right to block the pathway. This right in the public cannot be an easement, so we say that O or a predecessor in title has "dedicated" the land to the public. Closing the path for one day a year is one way that owners can rebut the presumption of dedication. Today, acquisition of land for public highways or other public rights of way is usually governed by statute.

## COVENANTS

We have seen that O, the owner of the fee simple, may dispose of all the rights and obligations of ownership by transferring the fee to A. O may also dispose of part of the rights — a grant to A of a life estate, with O retaining a reversion, for example. In both cases, O can limit these estates even further by attaching conditions to their retention. So O can convey to A a fee simple or life estate determinable with a grant "to A and heirs (or to A for life) as long as the property is used for church purposes". Or O can convey a fee simple or life estate subject to condition subsequent by a grant "to A and heirs (or to A for life) but if A sells liquor on the premises, O may re-enter and take possession". Both of these grants enable the grantor to retain control over the use of land, but only, as we have seen, by reclaiming the property.

Covenants provide an alternative way to control land use, and are especially useful for developers striving to increase the price of subdivision lots with promises of a certain quality of neighbourhood. Covenants are a private law alternative to municipal zoning laws, used to ensure, for example, that your neighbours do not fill their front yards with junked cars or pink flamingoes. If O, while retaining adjoining land, wants to sell a lot to A and wants to control A's activities on the land, O may exact a promise to that effect from A — a covenant. If A accepts a deed containing this covenant, then A's future use of the land is restricted by the promise. If A breaches the covenant, O's remedies in contract for damages are clear.

But what if O, having sold all the lots, is no longer interested in enforcing the covenant? Or what if B bought a lot in the same subdivision as A, and made the same covenant as A, but O now refuses to force B to abide by the rules. A will not have a remedy against B unless the covenant runs with the land; that is, unless the law permits A, and all of O's other grantees, to enjoy the benefit of the covenant made by all grantees to O, so that they will have the same rights to enforce the covenant as O, despite the lack of a contractual relationship among them.

Drafting covenants that will run with the land is not a task for the unprepared and imprecise. Consider the sale to A and B of Lots 41 and 42 respectively in a large development, O being the developer. Both grantees have covenanted in their deeds to build single-family dwellings to cost at least $500,000. Now let us suppose that instead of spending half a million dollars building a house, B parks a camper on Lot 42. Who will care? O, the developer, will, particularly if O has not yet sold the other lots; as will A, the next door neighbour; D, who bought the lot and camper from B; and C, who bought from A. We can diagram their relationship like this:

| **Lot 41** | **Lot 42** | |
|---|---|---|
| O | O | Covenantee (obtains benefit) |
| A | B | Covenantor (accepts burden) |
| C | D | Successors in Title |

Now who among these people can enforce B's covenant? Since there is privity of contract between O and B, O can always enforce the covenant. But it is O's successors, A and C, who care about B's camper, and their difficulties of enforcement are compounded by B's transfer of the property to D. Both A and C want to stop B from breaking the promise to O; in technical terms, they want the benefit of the covenant that B made to O to run to them.

At common law, O, the covenantee, could assign the benefit of a covenant relating to O's land to any successor in title who acquired the same estate in the land that O had had, if the covenant "touched and concerned the land of the covenantee". As you might expect, there has been considerable litigation on the meaning of a phrase as vague as "touches and concerns the land". As with easements, the covenant must benefit the land itself, as distinct from conferring a personal benefit to the covenantee; it must affect the use or value of the land. Also as with easements, the land to be benefitted must be near the land to be burdened, but need not adjoin it. If these conditions are met, the covenant runs with the land and, if O assigns the covenant to them, O's successors in title can enforce it against B. But what if B has sold the property to D? The running of the benefit will be of no use to A and A's successors in title if the burden of the covenant has not run to D.

Covenants can be either positive or negative. The distinction depends not on the wording but on the effect. A positive covenant requires a person to do something on the land, involving some expenditure, while a negative or restrictive covenant requires a person to refrain from using the land in a certain way. Neither at common law nor in equity does the burden of positive covenants run with the land. Thus, in the example above, A and A's successors in title have no rights against D, only against the original covenantor, B. This result is explicable only as part of a policy to promote free alienability of land. But as we shall see, equity permitted restrictions on free alienation if the grantee had accepted these as part of the grant. And equity provided an alternative doctrine for dealing with restrictive covenants, too.

Step back in time for a few moments to the mid-19th century, in the heart of London, England, where Mr. Tulk owned land in Leicester Square used as a garden and "pleasure ground". Tulk sold this property to Mr. Elms, who covenanted with Tulk to keep and maintain the land as a pleasure ground. Eventually, Mr. Moxhay acquired the property and started to build. Tulk sought an injunction to prevent the construction, claiming that the burden of the original covenant fastened onto the land and restricted its use. Moxhay responded that, as the assignee of a covenantor, he was not bound by what his predecessor in title had promised. The court had to accept Moxhay's defence; the precedents were clear. But the court found as fact that Moxhay knew about the covenant when he bought the land, even though the covenant was not included in the deed. So the court asked, not whether the covenant ran, but whether it accorded with principles of equity to permit a person who had bought with notice of a restrictive covenant to ignore the restrictions. In the result, Moxhay was compelled to abide by the covenant, and for many years thereafter, the case of *Tulk v. Moxhay* [1843-60] All E.R. Rep. 9, (1848) 41 E.R. 1143 (L.C.) was used as a precedent for enforcing the burden of restrictive covenants. Beware, however, of describing *Tulk v. Moxhay* as a precedent for permitting the burden of a covenant to run in equity in general. The court held that Moxhay had to abide by the restrictions because he had notice of them.

Over the years since the decision, and especially since the merger of the jurisdiction of the courts of common law and equity, judges have built on the notice basis of *Tulk v. Moxhay*. It is now safe to say that where a covenantor has given a promise in relation to land purchased from the covenantee, and this promise directly affects land retained by the covenantee, and both covenantor and covenantee intend that it run with the land, then the covenant becomes attached in equity to each parcel of land, and will follow each into the hands of successors in title to the covenantor and be enforceable against them unless they had no notice of the covenant. The notice requirement has thus changed from being the establishing force of the "running" to a mere prerequisite to its enforcement.

Now the circle should be complete. Benefits run at common law to successors in title to the covenantee and burdens "run" in equity to successors in title of the covenantor, if they have notice of the covenant. But recall that the covenant in *Tulk v. Moxhay* was in essence a promise not to do something, in other words, a negative or restrictive covenant. The covenantor was not required to "do" anything but was prohibited from doing something. This aspect of *Tulk v. Moxhay* has been used to limit its application; hence, for the burden of a covenant to "run," even in equity (remember, it cannot run at all at common law), the covenant must be negative in substance. If the covenantor promises to do something — build a house at a certain price, maintain a road, or pay a sum of money annually, for example — which requires "putting his hand in his pocket", the burden of these promises will not run. Hence the covenantee or successor will not be able to enforce this covenant against a successor in title of the covenantor at common law or in equity.

So far, we know that the successor in title to the covenantee can enforce the covenant because the benefit of the covenant runs with the land at common law. It runs as well in equity, if the covenant touches and concerns the land, in any of the following situations: the benefit of the covenant has somehow become annexed to the land; the benefit of the covenant has been assigned to the successor in title along with some estate in the land (not necessarily the same estate, as the common law required); or the covenant is part of a development plan or building scheme.

A development plan or building scheme involves a subdivision, and the court of equity, unencumbered by the logic of the common law, held that a development scheme is a special case demanding a special rule. Whether covenantors or successors in title bought into the development before or after the covenantee, the present possessor of the estate in the benefitted land is able to enforce the benefit of the covenant against any other owner in the development. To come within the special rule, the boundaries of the development must be well defined, and the developer must have intended the restrictions to apply to all the lots. A plot plan showing the restrictions is generally sufficient to meet these requirements. As well, both plaintiff and defendant must derive their titles from the developer.

In summary then, at common law, the benefit of covenants runs to successors in title to covenantees but the burden does not run to successors in title to the covenantor; at common law, the covenant is enforceable only against the person who first gave it. In equity, however, both the benefit and the burden will run, if the necessary conditions are met. One condition for the running of the burden is that the covenant must be negative in substance. Thus, a positive covenant is unenforceable at common law or in equity against a successor in title to the covenantor, because the burden would not run at common law and cannot "run" in equity under *Tulk v. Moxhay*.

Imagine, then, that the developer of a large subdivision agrees to install a swimming pool to increase sales. All those who buy agree to pay an annual levy to maintain this amenity. There is no question that they can be made to pay — they have promised to do so — but what happens when they decide to sell? The new owner is an assignee of a covenantor, and so the question is one of the running of a burden, regardless of who sues. As this is a positive covenant, the new owner can refuse to pay, even though it is manifestly unfair for the new owner to enjoy the amenity without contributing to its upkeep. Within the past few years, courts have been developing ways to exclude the non-payor. Developers could achieve this result by supplementing the covenant with other devices, such as creating a private recreation association to own the pool, and limiting access to those who pay a membership fee. Means to ensure that each owner in a condominium development contributes to the contingency fund will be discussed in Chapter Eleven.

# 8

# REVERSIONS, REMAINDERS AND THE LEGAL REMAINDER RULES

Before introducing the much-anticipated equitable interests in land, we must finish laying the foundation of rules developed by the common law courts for controlling the creation of interests and estates in land. So far, we have seen that O, the owner of a fee simple absolute, can divide this estate into lesser estates: life estates, fee tails, leasehold estates, and determinable estates or those subject to condition subsequent. The grantee can also create estates that will follow one another, with some coming into possession only after one or more preceding estates come to an end. An estate that is less than a fee simple is called a "particular estate" — it is only a particle of the potentially infinite circle. Estates that precede one another in a series are called "prior particular estates". If, in the same instrument, the grantor creates a series of estates, the ones following the first are called remainders, because the estate remains away from the grantor in the hands of grantees. As you may recall from Chapter Two, we call grantees of a remainder remainderpersons. In this chapter, we look more closely at the rules for creating valid remainders.

## REMAINDERS DISTINGUISHED FROM REVERSIONS

If the grantor does not create a remainder after a prior particular estate, the property reverts to the grantor or, if the grantor has died, to the grantor's estate. Reversions are not created by express grant but arise by implication from a grant of an estate that is less than a fee simple. If O grants a life estate to A and then, while A is still alive, decides to convey the fee simple to B, the conveyance is an assignment of the reversion. B gets the fee simple in reversion, subject to A's life estate. We do not call B's interest in the property a remainder, because a remainder must be created by the same instrument that created the prior particular estate.

## CONTINGENT REMAINDERS

Remainders may be vested or contingent. Suppose we have a grant to A for life, then in fee simple to B. A, the life tenant, is entitled to immediate possession of the property for her lifetime. B's fee simple is a vested remainder. It vests in interest at the effective date of the grant, and vests in possession when A dies. B can sell the fee simple subject to A's life estate. Compare this grant with a grant to A for life, then in fee simple to B when B is 21. B will get the fee simple only on reaching the age of 21. In technical language, B's interest is contingent and will vest in interest on B's 21st birthday. Anyone who buys B's interest before that date is buying, not a fee simple, but the chance of getting a fee simple if B lives to be 21.

Thus, if the only thing standing between the grantee and possession of a remainder is a prior particular estate, the remainder is vested in interest, and will vest in possession at the end of the prior particular estate. But if there are conditions that must be met before the grantee is entitled to claim the remainder, then it is a contingent remainder, subject to a condition precedent. The grantee has no estate until the condition is met, allowing the remainder to vest. It vests in interest when the condition is met, which may be earlier than the end of the prior particular estate, and therefore earlier than the vesting in possession.

There are two different kinds of uncertainty that make a remainder contingent. If the grantor has identified a particular grantee, we will know who, if anyone, will receive the estate identified in the grant. But if the grantor has imposed conditions precedent, it is not certain that the identified grantee will actually get the estate. Conditions may be something that only the grantee can do — reach the age of 21, graduate at the top of the class, join the Presbyterian Church, become Prime Minister. Or they may be conditions over which the grantee has no control — "to A if my daughter has no children" or "to A if my daughter becomes a bankrupt".

It is also possible to create grants in which we cannot identify initially the particular person or persons who will meet the requirements for taking an estate. For example, when property is left to C for life with a remainder to the children of A then living, we will not be able to identify the remainderpersons until C has died, for no one knows in advance whether A will have children and which ones will be alive at C's death. The estate to the remainderpersons, then, cannot vest until the end of the prior particular estate, when it will vest in interest and possession at the same time.

Similarly, a conveyance "to A for life and then to A's first son and heirs" will create a present life estate in A, and the possibility of a fee simple in remainder to A's first son. (You need not worry about the Rule in *Shelley's Case* (1581), 1 Co. Rep. 93b here, because the remainder is to a specific person, not the whole line of succession.) Whether the remainder is vested or contingent at the effective date of the grant depends on whether A has already produced a son. If A has, there are no conditions attached and the grant is therefore vested in interest, although it will not vest in possession until A's death. If A has no son, then the remainder is contingent and will vest in interest only on a son being born.

One grant can combine both kinds of uncertainties — in a grant "to A for life and then in fee simple to A's first son if he graduates from law school", for example. Here, once A has a son, we know who might meet the condition precedent, but the remainder is contingent until he does.

Suppose that the condition is not met and the grantee's interest never vests. Who, then, becomes the owner? Looking at the previous example, it will not be the life tenant or the life tenant's heirs, because the grantor gave A only a life estate. Nor can it be the remainderperson, because he has not met the condition. There is only one alternative left and that is for the fee simple to revert to O, or, if O is dead, to O's estate. Thus, a grant of a contingent remainder in fee simple also creates — if the remainder does not vest within the time permitted — the chance of a reversion. Do not confuse this chance with the possibility of reverter that the grantor retains when granting a determinable estate, or the right of re-entry that the grantor retains when granting an estate subject to condition subsequent. Reversions and reverters are both reversionary interests in the grantor, but the terms refer to quite different interests and cannot be used interchangeably.

The grantor can provide for another outcome if the contingent remainder does not vest by providing in the same instrument for an alternative contingent remainder — a remainder to a different person if the condition for the first remainder is not met. For example, with a grant "to A for life and then in fee simple to A's first daughter to graduate from law school, and if none does, then in fee simple to A's children in equal shares as tenants in common", A has a life estate, A's first daughter to graduate from law school has a contingent remainder in fee simple, and A's children have an alternative contingent remainder in fee simple, conditional on A's having no daughter who graduates from law school. Alternative remainders are always contingent because they are subject to the condition precedent of the first remainder failing to vest.

By now you should be wondering how long we will wait before we decide that the contingent remainder will never vest. If the condition is one that can be satisfied only within the grantee's lifetime, such as reaching the age of 21 or graduating from law school, we know that the condition must be met, if at all, within the grantee's lifetime. But not all conditions are of this sort. Some contingent remainders are contingent because the grantee will not be ascertained until the death of the life tenant — the holder of the prior particular estate. As will be explained below, it is the life tenant's life, not the life of the grantee, that sets the time limit for vesting.

# THE LEGAL REMAINDER RULES

The legal remainder rules were developed by the courts of common law to address two concerns: setting the time limit within which a contingent remainder must vest in interest, if it is ever to, and preventing gaps in seisin. Before going on, you might find it helpful to review the discussion of seisin in Chapter Two. In feudal times, the lord needed to know who was seised of an estate in land, in order to identify the person who was liable for feudal services and incidents. After enactment of the statute *Quia Emptores, 1290* (U.K.), 18 Edw. 1, c. 1, enabled holders of estates in land to transfer those estates during their lifetimes without obtaining permission of the lord, courts developed rules to restrict attempts to impose conditions on transfers that would create uncertainty as to who was next in line for the property. Hence we have the legal remainder rules, which developed somewhat haphazardly but which remain valid in most common law jurisdictions today, setting limits on the creation of future interests.

Most texts identify four legal remainder rules, although not all texts present them in the same order. Some of the rules apply only to contingent remainders, some to all remainders. But all of the remainder rules apply only to interests created at common law. We call these interests "legal interests" in order to distinguish them from the "equitable interests" and "legal executory interests" that we will learn about in the next chapter. To be a remainder, the legal interest must be created in the same instrument that creates a prior particular estate. Equivalent property rights to remainders can be created, for example, by a grant of a life estate to A, and, in a separate instrument, the assignment of the grantor's reversion to B. In this case, however, B does not have a remainder and the remainder rules do not apply.

## Rule One: No Remainders After a Fee Simple

The first two rules that we look at deal with the kind of estates that can support a remainder. The first rule follows from *Quia Emptores* and is really part of the definition of a remainder. Since a remainder is preceded by a particular estate — an estate granted in the same instrument that is less than a fee simple — there cannot be a remainder after a fee simple. This rule does not distinguish among absolute fee simples, determinable fee simples or fee simples subject to condition subsequent. Remainders are prohibited after all three. But the rule that there cannot be a remainder after a fee does not prevent a remainder after a life estate or even a fee tail, so that one can create a series of life estates.

## Rule Two: No Springing Freeholds

The second rule follows from the requirement that there can be no abeyance of seisin. Thus, grantors who wanted to create remainders to vest in interest in the future first had to create a freehold in someone else, who could hold the seisin until it could be transferred to the remainderperson. In technical language, a contingent freehold interest is void unless it is supported by a prior particular estate of freehold. Stated more metaphorically, this rule prohibits freeholds that spring from the grantor to the remainderperson at some point in the future; it prevents gaps in seisin.

Thus a grant of a fee simple to A when A marries, if A is still single, transfers nothing to A, because a common law grant requires an immediate transfer of seisin. Since A has not met the condition for receiving the grant, and may never meet it, there can be no transfer of seisin. So if O wants to provide for A in the future, O must transfer seisin to the holder of a prior particular estate of freehold (effectively, a life estate, since the fee tail has been abolished in most jurisdictions) with a contingent remainder to A, thus: "To B for life, and then to A and heirs when A marries". With this grant, seisin is transferred immediately to B, who has a life estate in possession, while A has a contingent remainder in fee. If A marries during B's lifetime, the contingent remainder will vest in interest then, and in possession on B's death, with seisin moving smoothly from B to A. If A does not marry within B's lifetime, the remainder fails, and the fee simple, and seisin, reverts to the grantor or the grantor's estate. See Rule Three.

What happens if the prior particular estate is a leasehold? Recall that the leaseholder does not have seisin — the leaseholder's estate, although possessory, is not a freehold. So a grant "to A for one year and then to B and heirs if B is 21" does not create a valid contingent remainder to an underage B. The lease to A is valid, but seisin remains with the grantor's estate, which retains the fee simple in reversion. But if B is already 21, B's interest is vested, not contingent. B gets a fee simple, but not immediate possession, because the fee simple is subject to the one-year lease. There is no springing freehold; with the condition met, seisin is transferred immediately to B.

Remember that B gets seisin in this example because B's interest is not contingent: the conditions were satisfied at the effective date of the grant, and B gets seisin then. It is appropriate, then, to describe this state of title as a fee simple in B subject to a leasehold for a term of one year in A; it would also be correct to describe it as a leasehold in A with a vested remainder in fee simple in B. Remember, then, that Rule Two does not prohibit estates that will not vest in possession until some time in the future; it prohibits vesting in interest in the future unless the grantor has already transferred seisin in the same instrument which creates the remainder with a grant of a prior particular estate of freehold.

Look again at the wording of the rule. If the contingent grant is of a leasehold rather than a freehold, then it need not be supported by a prior particular estate of freehold. So, a grant "to A for 999 years when A gets married" is valid, because seisin remains with the grantor during a lease, and will not, therefore, spring to A when A marries and the leasehold interest vests.

## Rule Three: Timely Vesting and Class Closing

The third rule is also a rule against gaps in seisin. As noted above, we will not wait later than the end of the preceding life tenancy for a remainder to vest. If, at the death of the life tenant, the remainderperson or persons are not ascertained and all conditions met so that possession and seisin can pass to them immediately, the remainder fails. Stated technically, a remainder is void unless it vests in interest by the end of the prior particular estate. This rule, particularly in American texts, is sometimes referred to as the doctrine of destructibility of contingent remainders.

As we have seen, where O has conveyed Blackacre "to A for life, remainder to A's first son and heirs when he is 21", A has a present vested life estate and A's first son, if any, has a contingent remainder in fee simple that will vest in interest on his 21st birthday. If the first son is not 21 when A dies, the remainder fails and the property reverts to O or O's estate. But suppose that A's first son is 19 when A dies. Since O intended that the son receive the fee simple at 21, why not have the estate revert to O to hold until then, then have it go to the son? Because that would deprive the lord of the incident of wardship. The legal remainder rules are not concerned with the grantor's intentions but with keeping clear who has seisin, and preventing evasion of feudal services and incidents. Upon A's death, his son being only 19, O or O's estate gets the reversion in fee simple and keeps it. For the estate to go to the son two years later, according to the intent of the grant, seisin would have to spring from O or O's estate to the son. But springing freeholds are prohibited; the remainder can vest in interest only during A's lifetime. O can, of course, make a new grant to the son when he is 21, but then, at least prior to *Quia Emptores*, the lord would be able to collect a fine.

As long as A held seisin in the above example, we would wait to see if the condition would be met in A's lifetime. If it is, then the remainder is no longer contingent but vested in interest, to vest in possession when the life tenant dies. Remembering that the legal remainder rules are concerned with gaps in seisin as well as timely vesting will help in recognizing the remainders that are void *ab initio* because of Rule Three. For example, a grantor might grant land to A for life and a remainder in fee to those who send flowers to A's funeral, or a remainder to those who attain majority after A's death, or a remainder to B and heirs one year (or one day) after A's death. What these examples have in common is that the remainder cannot possibly vest during A's lifetime or at the moment of A's death, so it is not permitted to vest at all. The grantees of the attempted remainder to those who sent flowers, for example, cannot be ascertained until after A dies — beyond the time permitted for vesting. The remainder is thus void *ab initio*.

What happens when the remainderpersons are the members of a class, such as "my grandchildren", "the top student in the graduating class at the law school for the ten years following my death", "the children of B", or other people who are not named but are part of an identifiable group? Consider, for example, a grant "to A for life and on A's death, to B's children and heirs". Suppose that when O makes the grant, B is dead, survived by three children. Those children receive a vested remainder in fee simple, with possession deferred until the end of the life estate. Now suppose, instead, that B is alive but has no children. The remainderpersons, B's as yet unborn children, get a contingent remainder, contingent on their being born, when their interest will vest. A gets a life estate, and O's estate gets a reversion in fee simple, contingent on B having no children at A's death. Suppose now that B, at O's death, has two children, X and Y. Since the children are ascertained and there are no conditions precedent to their taking their estate, they have a vested remainder in fee simple and O's estate has nothing. Because the remainder is vested, if X or Y die before A, their share of the fee simple will go to their estate.

But now suppose that before A dies, B has another child, Z. As O intended that all of B's children were to share in the property, it becomes necessary to decrease the share of the estate that has already vested in interest in X and Y so that Z can share, too. X and Y do not lose their vested remainder, but it is no longer worth as much. We say that X and Y have vested remainders subject to partial divestment if other grantees join the class. Under the rule in *Festing v. Allen* (1843), 152 E.R. 1204 (Exch.), however, the class closes at the end of the prior particular estate, when the remainder vests in possession. Thus, any of B's children born after A's death will not be able to share in the property. The class closing rule is qualified by the rule in *Reeve v. Long* (1694), 1 Salk. 227, 89 E.R. 381, which extends the period permitted for vesting by the gestation period if, at the end of the prior particular estate, a woman is expecting a baby that would belong to the class if it is born alive.

## Rule Four: No Shifting Freeholds

We have seen that estates can follow one another in orderly progression, so that, for example, O can convey "to A for life and on A's death, to B and heirs". B's fee simple in remainder vests in interest from the effective date of the grant but B or B's estate has to wait until A dies for the fee simple to vest in possession. Suppose however, that O wants to convey to A for life but wants to ensure that if A does not behave as O wants, A will lose the property and it will either come back to O or go to B. For example, O conveys "to A for life but if A goes bankrupt, then to B and heirs". This grant creates a condition subsequent and, if valid, would shift the freehold from A to B on the happening of the condition. But such a shift is not permitted and the attempt to create a remainder in B is void for the following reasons.

First, a remainder comes into possession only on the natural termination of the prior particular estate, and natural termination means the death of the life tenant or, with a determinable estate, happening of the determining circumstance. Second, recall from our discussion of conditional estates that an interest following on the breach of a condition, whether a possibility of reverter or right of re-entry, was a reversionary interest that belonged only to the grantor. Thus, while O might create an estate in A subject to the condition that if A became bankrupt O might re-enter, at common law O could not give this right to another grantee. Similarly, O could get the property back automatically on breach of the condition if O created a determinable estate with a possibility of reverter. But the property would go back to O or O's estate; no outsider to the grant could benefit from it. Rule Four can also be expressed as no conditions in strangers.

If we were dealing with attempts to create a remainder after a fee simple determinable or subject to condition subsequent, the remainder would be void because of Rule One: No remainder after a fee simple. But since it is also possible to create life estates that are determinable or subject to condition subsequent, we have Rule Four: A remainder is void if it is designed to take effect by cutting short a prior particular estate. Expressed positively, Rule Four requires a remainder to take effect only on the natural termination of the prior particular estate.

Recall that one distinction between the determinable estate and the estate subject to condition subsequent is in the conceptualization of the limitation. With determinable estates, it defines the duration of the estate; with estates subject to condition subsequent, it is something added. Thus, while the determinable life estate and the life estate subject to condition subsequent will both terminate naturally on the death of the life tenant, the determinable estate has an alternative natural termination point — the occurrence of the event that changes the possibility of reverter into a reality and automatically returns the estate to the grantor. Thus, although there can be no remainder after a life estate subject to condition subsequent, it is possible, with careful drafting, to create a valid remainder after a determinable life estate.

Remember, however, that the legal remainder rules apply only to legal estates. If one creates equitable estates, by first conveying the property to a trustee, it is possible to create estates that are generally immune from the remainder rules, and therefore to create interests that would be void if one attempted to create them as legal remainders. We now turn to the developments that make this possible.

# 9

# EQUITABLE ESTATES, THE STATUTE OF USES AND THE MODERN TRUST

The common law rules regarding the passage of seisin were not intended to facilitate conveyancing. Indeed, until *Quia Emptores, 1290* (U.K.), 18 Edw. 1, c. 1, and the *Statute of Wills, 1540* (U.K.), 32 Hen. 8, c. 1, property owners had quite limited power to alienate their property. And the requirement for a physical ritual of feoffment by livery of seisin meant that land transfers could not be conducted in the most convenient place, or with any secrecy, but had to be done publicly on the land itself. So conveyancers developed the equitable estate in order to create and transfer estates in land without having to transfer seisin.

This is how it worked. Legal title, recognized by the common law courts, was conveyed to a trusted person, called a "feoffee to uses", who held it for the use of another. Seisin was transferred along with legal title to the feoffee to uses, who held the property on the instructions of the grantor and for the use and benefit of the grantor or some other person whom the grantor named. In law French, the person who was entitled to the benefit of the property was called the *cestui que use*, from "*cestui a que use le feoffment fuit fait*". *Cestui que usent* (the plural form; *usent* is a verb) were not recognized as having any rights in the common law courts, but they could enforce the obligations of the feoffee in the court of equity. Hence, their interest in the property became known as "equitable title".

## SEPARATION OF LEGAL AND EQUITABLE TITLE

With recognition of the equitable estate, it became possible to split freehold or leasehold estates so that title to the estate was divided between two people, while preserving the estate as a fee simple or life estate or whatever else it had been. Up to now, we have taken the circle of the fee simple and divided it into parts so that if A receives a life estate, then O no longer has a full fee simple but a part only, called a reversion. Now visualize the circle as a coin lying flat on the table. If you cut the coin into wedges, the wedges represent very different estates. Some may be particular estates such as a life estate or a fee tail, and one will be either a reversion or a remainder. Put together, the particular estates and the reversion or remainder form the whole coin. Thus, if O gives one piece of the coin to A as a life estate and the other piece by the same conveyance to B, B has a remainder in fee simple, and A and B together own all the component wedges.

Imagine now that the coin, instead of lying flat on the table, stands on its edge. Now split it into two circles by cutting it straight through from edge to edge, so that what you have is one coin with a heads side only and another with a tails side only. We have now divided the fee simple into two estates that are each full circles — each is still a fee simple that can be divided into particular estates and remainders or reversions. We have divided the legal fee simple from the equitable fee simple, and in the process, freed the equitable fee simple from the common law rules. All of this makes the doctrine of estates much more flexible and useful. With seisin firmly in the hands of the person who has the legal freehold estate, conveyancers could do many things, especially with regard to future interests, that were not possible if they had to worry about a continuous passage of seisin or a livery of seisin.

From at least the 14th century, it was fairly common in some parts of England to convey, by livery of seisin, to the use of another. Knights who left on the Crusades conveyed legal title to their trusted friends to hold while they were away, for the use of the knight or the knight's dependants. Thus, if the knight died before his son was old enough to take over, the feoffee to uses would protect the estate from the lord's claims to feudal incidents such as wardship. With a conveyance to the use, the grantor, if he could trust his grantees, would continue to enjoy the fruits and profits of the land without the responsibilities of ownership.

But what if the grantor had chosen feoffees to uses who proved untrustworthy and took the benefits of ownership for themselves? So far as the common law courts were concerned, the total control of the land lay in the person who had been enfeoffed by livery of seisin. Since the feoffees to uses had seisin, they had everything. So if *cestui que usent*, whether the grantor or other named beneficiaries, did not receive the benefits expected, all they could say by way of complaint was that the grantee was ignoring the purpose for which the grant was made. To this, the common law courts said: "Perhaps true, but irrelevant. As far as we are concerned, this grantee received a freehold estate by livery of seisin and so received title, seisin and the right to possession. The grantor gave away the full circle of the fee simple and so has nothing left. So neither the grantor nor the beneficiaries who claim through the grantor have legal rights that we can recognize, protect and enforce."

Despite the common law courts' refusal to intervene if the feoffee to uses denied the *cestui que use* the profits or possession of the property, or even transferred the estate to someone else, conveyances to uses proliferated. They were wonderfully useful for avoiding feudal obligations, for circumventing the rules of primogeniture, for providing separate estates for married women that would not come under the control of their husbands, and, since widows could claim dower rights only in legal estates, for shielding property from dower claims. Also, since seisin stayed with the holder of the legal title, grantors could use conveyances to the uses to avoid the legal remainder rules and create the springing and shifting interests that were void at common law.

But feoffees to uses were not entirely free from supervision. Those who proved untrustworthy could be held to their obligations by the Chancellor in the Court of Chancery (also called the court of equity). This court developed alongside the common law courts out of the Chancellor's responsibilities as keeper of the King's conscience. The Chancellor heard people's petitions to the King when things had not gone their way in the common law courts, and sometimes offered a remedy when the strictness of the common law rules perpetrated an injustice in a particular situation. And what could be more unjust than to leave unpunished feoffees to uses who had betrayed the trust and confidence put in them by landowners and vulnerable *cestui que usent*?

Of course, until the merger of the jurisdiction of the courts of common law and equity in the late 19th century, equity could not interfere directly with a decision in a legal dispute between competing claimants to property. But the Chancellor had jurisdiction over the body and mind of the subject. To ensure that the common law did not permit people to renege on obligations willingly accepted, the Chancellor issued orders to individuals (what today we call "injunctions"), to act according to the dictates of good conscience. So where A had accepted the fee simple in Blackacre on the understanding that A was to hold the estate for the benefit of O, or for someone else named by O, the Chancellor would see that A lived up to the understanding by providing a remedy to *cestui que usent*.

It became accepted practice, then, on the failure of feoffees to uses to abide by the terms of the conveyance, for the injured party to obtain an order from the Chancellor directing the feoffee to uses to hold the property for the benefit of *cestui que usent* or to convey the legal estate directly to *cestui que usent*. Practice developed into precedent and by the end of the 15th century most of the land of England was held for the use of another. Conveyances to the use split the fee simple into two superimposed circles. One, labelled the "legal fee simple", went to the feoffee to uses; it is as round as when O had it but only half as deep. The other, labelled the "equitable fee simple", remained in O or went to *cestui que usent* named by O. Feoffees to uses, so far as the common law is concerned, have a full circle. *Cestui que usent* have a full circle in the court of equity.

The Chancellor's willingness to enforce the promises made by feoffees to uses altered dramatically the content of the bundle of rights and obligations that come with ownership of a legal fee simple, so that it became possible to say that the feoffee to uses was the legal owner of the fee simple in Blackacre, while the *cestui que use* was the beneficial or equitable owner. In a conveyance to uses, the person who held the legal estate was the only one who had the right to bring a real action in the common law courts; *cestui que usent* had only a personal right to seek help from the court of equity. But feoffees to uses were titular owners only, for *cestui que usent* could force them to do with the land what O had planned from the beginning.

Since the person who held equitable title did not have seisin, *cestui que usent* could convey their equitable estates without the inconvenience and publicity of livery of seisin. Eventually, so too could the owner of the legal estate. Suppose O did not go through a livery of seisin with A but merely signed a contract — a deed — conveying Blackacre to A and accepting the purchase price. If O then reneged on the contract, A could sue for damages for breach of contract, but A could not bring a real action in the common law courts to compel O to give up possession of the land. A did not have seisin because there had been no livery of seisin, and real actions were available only to the person seised. But for a number of reasons — including A's desire to have the land, procedural barriers to bringing an action for damages for breach of contract, or O's having already squandered the purchase money — A might not be satisfied with an action for the return of the purchase price. So A would take the tale of woe to the Chancellor who, if he believed A, would order O to hold the land for the benefit or the use of A.

It was but a short step from this result to a widespread practice of conveying not by livery of seisin but by execution of an agreement of purchase and sale. Once the purchase price had been paid, the agreement would be regarded in the court of equity as a transfer of the equitable title. Since equitable title carried significant rights in the court of equity, it mattered not that the grantor retained legal title. Because O purported to sell and A paid the price agreed upon, the label attached to this transaction was "bargain and sale".

By the end of the 15th century, then, there were three common ways of creating an equitable estate or, in the language of the time, raising a use. The earliest common method, as we have just seen, was by a feoffment to uses. O would, by livery of seisin, convey Blackacre to A and heirs for the use of O and heirs or B and heirs. At law, A was the owner in fee simple, and at equity O or B was the owner. Second, the bargain and sale transaction would place the grantee in the position of holding the equitable title while the grantor retained only the legal title. Third, where

O conveyed by deed to A and in that deed covenanted "to stand seised" to the use of A and heirs, if O and A were related by either blood or marriage, then the Chancellor would order that, as in the case of bargain and sale, while O retained the legal title through failure of livery, A had the equitable title.

One caveat: the Chancellor would not use his jurisdiction to the disadvantage of the *bona fide* purchaser for value without notice — a person sometimes referred to as "equity's darling". So if the feoffee to uses conveyed legal title by livery of seisin to someone who paid market value for the property, without knowledge that the conveyance was a breach of obligations of a feoffee to uses, the court of equity could give the *cestui que use* a personal remedy against the feoffee to uses, but would not order the innocent purchaser to give up possession of the land.

## ENDING THE SEPARATION WITH THE *STATUTE OF USES*

Recall that various peculiar rules have been explained as part of the ongoing struggle to avoid or to collect feudal obligations. Since many of the feudal incidents attached to fairly commonplace events of life, such as a father dying before his children were of age, or children wishing to marry the person of their choosing, a conveyance to a feoffee to uses who had no children could deprive the lord of revenue. And since mesne lords, after *Quia Emptores*, were gradually eliminated, so that by the time of Henry VIII most feudal obligations were owed directly to the Crown, it was the King, not the lords, who suffered most from the evasion of feudal incidents. King Henry VIII, as historians, playwrights and novelists tell us, had his troubles; and conveyances to uses were reducing his income just as his expenses increased. When Parliament refused to vote him more money, he turned his attention to recovering the lost feudal incidents.

Earlier attempts to control conveyances to uses had produced legislation to prevent their use to defraud creditors or to evade the mortmain statutes. Now Henry VIII proposed to eliminate conveyances to uses altogether, by the simple expedient of a statute that would re-unite legal and equitable title in the hands of *cestui que usent*. Henceforth, a conveyance to uses would give the benefits of the property to the person for whom the grantor intended them, but that person would also receive seisin and the obligations of estate ownership.

Henry VIII could not govern without the consent of Parliament, where he was none too popular. But Parliament was full of common law lawyers, who did not like conveyancing work being handled by the Chancery bar. So they accepted Henry's proposal and in 1535 passed the *Statute of Uses, 1535* (U.K.), 27 Hen. 8, c. 10, to take effect in 1536.

Although repealed in England in 1925, the *Statute of Uses* was part of the received law of the Canadian common law jurisdictions and it, perhaps in a re-enacted version, is a key part of Canadian land law today. The operative section, a marvel of soporific repetition, can be summarized thus: where any person or persons is seised of any interest in land to the use, confidence, or trust of any other person, persons, or body politick, the person, persons or body politick who is to benefit from the use shall henceforth stand and be seised of the same estate in law as they had in equity; and the estate given to the person who stood seised to the use of another shall be deemed to be in the person, persons, or body politick who is to benefit from the use.

Thus, where, prior to the *Statute of Uses*, O conveyed "to A and heirs for the use of B and heirs", the state of the title was clear. A had a legal fee simple and B an equitable fee simple. A was seised to the use of another, B. The effect of the Statute is to drop A from the grant and move seisin to B. B now becomes the owner in fee simple of both the equitable estate, by the terms of the grant, and the legal estate, by the operation of the *Statute of Uses*. This process is called "executing the use". A is being written out, as it were, and B's interest is increased by the addition of A's.

The complete process involves two steps: first, the raising of a use and splitting of legal and equitable title by the conveyance; and second, the re-uniting of legal and equitable title when the Statute executes the use. Where O enfeoffs A and heirs to the use of B and heirs, the Statute cannot work until A gets the estate and is seised to the use of B. In a sense, therefore, A must have the estate long enough for the Statute to work on it and execute the use. In conveyances to uses that are executed by the *Statute of Uses*, the feoffee to uses will get the estate for a split second — a scintilla of time — then lose it to the various *cestui que usent*.

Sometimes surprising things can happen during that second, as *Pimbe's Case* (1585), 72 E.R. 528 illustrates. There, after committing treason, A received a conveyance of land from O, to the use of B. B then sold his interest to C. Once A was convicted of treason, any land of which A was seised at the time of the treason or thereafter was forfeited to the Crown. In the split second that A was seised of the legal estate before the *Statute of Uses* executed the use, the estate went to the Crown. Poor C had to accept that B had nothing to sell to C, as B had received nothing. But there is a happy ending — the monarch presented the land to C as an act of grace.

There then is the *Statute of Uses*. It seems brilliantly simple and straightforward, but within a century, conveyancers and courts had developed enough ways around the Statute that it failed utterly to eliminate conveyances to uses. Indeed, it may have given them new life by creating the possibility of interests in land previously unrecognized at common law or in equity.

## CONVEYANCES TO USES THAT BLOCK THE *STATUTE OF USES*

Recall that the Statute applies only where a person is seised of property to the use of another; that is, where the feoffee to uses has been granted a present freehold estate. Giving the feoffee to uses a leasehold estate thus protected the uses from the Statute. The estate in the *cestui que usent* cannot be greater than the estate given to the feoffee to uses, but, for most purposes, a grant to A for 999 years to the use of B for 999 years is almost as valuable to B as an equitable fee simple.

One could also block the Statute with a conveyance to a corporation. When describing *cestui que usent*, the Statute mentions persons or bodies politick — but persons only when referring to feoffees to uses. Bodies politick in this context means artificial persons — corporations or other legal entities that are treated as natural persons for the purposes of owning property. If the feoffee to uses was a corporation, the Statute was thus avoided, the uses were not executed, and the corporation retained the legal title subject to the obligations to the *cestui que use*.

A third way of blocking the Statute was to give feoffees to uses active duties to perform. Judicial interpretation of the Statute limited it to bare uses, where feoffee to uses did nothing but hold seisin. If, instead, feoffees to uses had to manage the property and pay the rents and profits to *cestui que usent*, the separation of legal and equitable title was maintained, for without legal title the feoffees to uses would be unable to carry out their responsibilities.

## CONVEYANCES TO USES THAT EXHAUST THE *STATUTE OF USES*

Evading the Statute by creating grants that the Statute only partly executed was not as straightforward as blocking its operation completely and so took a little longer to gain judicial acceptance. However, within a century and a half of passage of the *Statute of Uses*, it was possible, by adding a few words to a conveyance, to achieve what had been possible with a conveyance to uses prior to the Statute. One factor in this development was passage of the *Statute of Tenures, 1660*, (U.K.), 12 Car. 2, c. 24, discussed in Chapter One, which, by abolishing feudal incidents, removed some of the significance of the *Statute of Uses* for the Crown.

In the early years after passage of the Statute, neither the common law courts nor the Chancellor would enforce a use on a use. A conveyance from O "to A and heirs to the use of B and heirs to the use of C and heirs" was interpreted as giving A the legal fee simple for a scintilla of time. Then the Statute executed the use and gave A's legal fee simple to B, who already had the equitable fee simple by the grant. Having both sides of the full fee simple, B had all that O had to grant and there was nothing left for C. The words of grant to C were treated as inconsistent with the rest of the grant, and ignored. But after passage of the *Statute of Tenures*, the court of equity began to interpret this grant so as to give some meaning to all its words. The grant of the legal estate to A to the use of B was still executed, so that B got both legal and equitable title. But now the courts ruled that B held legal title for the benefit of C, so equitable title moved from B to C — but equitable title only. The Statute, having executed the first use of the fee simple to B, was exhausted and did not execute the second use of the fee simple to C.

Note that we are dealing not with all uses on a use, but with a use of a fee simple on a use of a fee simple. There is a difference between a use on a use and a use after a use. The Statute will execute fully a grant from O "to A and heirs to the use of B for life, and then to the use of C and heirs". Because C's use of a fee simple follows after B's use of a life estate, it is not a use upon a use. The Statute will execute any number of successive life estates; it is exhausted only by executing a use of a fee simple. Similarly, the Statute will execute fully a grant from O "to A and heirs to the use of B for life, then to the use of C and heirs if C is then 21, but if C is not, then to the use of D and heirs". Here there is only one equitable fee simple, given either to C or to D. If C meets the condition precedent, C will get the equitable estate by the grant and the legal estate by operation of the *Statute of Uses*; if C does not meet the condition, D gets both the equitable and legal fee simple.

Return now to the grant of a use on a use: "to A and heirs to the use of B and heirs to the use of C and heirs". Once courts allowed the second use in fee simple to C, it became possible to eliminate B from the grant. Start with a grant "to A and heirs to the use of A of heirs", which was interpreted as giving A the legal fee simple to hold for the benefit of A. Regardless of the effect of the *Statute of Uses*, A would have both legal and equitable title. Now add another fee simple to this grant, so that it reads "to A and heirs to the use of A and heirs to the use of C and heirs". The use to C is a use upon the first use to A, so it is not executed by the Statute. But A was required to give up equitable title to C, since by the grant A was to hold the estate for the use of C. The cumbersome "to A and heirs to the use of A and heirs" was shortened to "Unto and to the use of A and heirs" which meant the same thing, and *voilà* — you had a form of conveyance with which to separate legal and equitable estates almost as if the *Statute of Uses* had not been passed.

## THE *STATUTE OF USES* AND TRANSFERRING TITLE TO LAND

As we have seen, with equity's protection of claims of *cestui que usent*, the common law method of transferring an estate in land by livery of seisin was supplanted by transfers of the equitable estate arising from a feoffment to uses, the bargain and sale deed, or a covenant to stand seised. After passage of the *Statute of Uses*, when O agreed to sell to A and A paid the purchase price, the Statute executed the use thus raised in A, so that A got the equitable estate by the bargain and sale and the legal estate by the operation of the *Statute of Uses*. Thus, A had the complete fee simple, but without the public ceremony of livery of seisin.

The drafters of the *Statute of Uses* had anticipated this result, so when the Statute became effective, Parliament also passed the *Statute of Enrolments, 1535* (U.K.), 27 Hen. 8, c. 16, requiring grantees to record, on payment of a substantial fee, all bargains and sales of freehold interests in land. But the *Statute of Enrolments*, like the *Statute of Uses*, applied only to conveyances of freeholds, so conveyancers and the courts developed a way around it. O would, by bargain and sale, grant A a leasehold estate for a term of years. At common law, the lease would not be valid until the lessee took possession, but the deed of bargain and sale was sufficient to transfer an equitable estate. Then, in a separate deed, O would release the equitable reversion to A. Since it was not a bargain and sale, the release did not have to be recorded. By the doctrine of merger, explained in Chapter Two, A's leasehold would be subsumed in the fee simple acquired by the release, and A would have a present vested fee simple absolute in equity, to which would be added the legal estate and seisin, by the operation of the *Statute of Uses*.

Eventually this two-step process, called a "lease and release," was combined in one document, and it remained the standard way to convey a fee simple until legislation validated transfers of freehold estates without livery of seisin. Today, O can convey directly to A in fee by deed and, though it still exists as a possible way to convey a freehold estate in some jurisdictions, livery has disappeared as a requirement.

Had it not been circumvented by the lease and release, the *Statute of Enrolments* would have greatly simplified land transfers in England, for all of the documents relating to a particular property would be recorded in a public office rather than being held by the estate owners or their solicitors. Most of the colonial legislatures provided for registration of land transactions early on, when the chain of title contained little more than the original Crown grants. But it was only in the late 20th century that some jurisdictions passed legislation mandating standard short forms for conveyancing, so that O could grant an estate to A using relatively straightforward verbs and nouns such as "grants in fee simple" without having to include a recital of phrases like bargain and sale and lease and release.

## THE *STATUTE OF USES* AND TESTAMENTARY DISPOSITIONS

In the first few years after its passage, the *Statute of Uses* was effective in preventing the use of conveyances to uses to make what were in effect testamentary dispositions. Prior to the Statute, O would enfeoff A to the use of O for O's lifetime, and then to the use of named beneficiaries on the terms and conditions that O specified to A. Loss of this power created such unrest that in 1540 Henry VIII agreed to passage of the *Statute of Wills*, recognizing the right of property owners to dispose by will of all their lands held in soccage tenure, and two-thirds of their lands held in knight service. Judges tended to interpret broadly the powers of disposition given in the *Statute of Wills*, so that it was possible in wills to grant a fee simple without using the magic words of limitation "and heirs". In addition, devises did not have to comply with the legal remainder rules, since they were treated as creating executory interests, regardless of whether the words of the devise expressly raised a use. To understand the implications for conveyancing of this judicial choice, we need to look more closely at executory interests.

## THE *STATUTE OF USES* AND EXECUTORY INTERESTS

Recall that the legal remainder rules applied only to legal remainders. Before passage of the *Statute of Uses*, one of the advantages of a conveyance to uses was that, with seisin firmly in the hands of the feoffee to uses, one could grant equitable estates that would spring in the future from the grantor to a grantee. One could wait as long as necessary for contingent interests to vest — the wait-and-see period did not end with the end of the prior particular estate. At common law, O could grant a determinable fee simple or fee simple subject to condition subsequent and retain a possibility of reverter or a right of re-entry, but could not provide for the fee simple to shift to another grantee on breach of the condition. Nor could O grant a remainder to take effect on the unnatural termination of a life estate subject to condition subsequent. But when dealing with equitable estates, the court of equity ignored all these rules, which, after all, would have interfered with the ability of feoffees to uses to carry out the grantor's intentions.

Prior to 1536, then, so long as O used a conveyance to uses, O could create interests that would be void at common law. For example, if O granted "to X and heirs for the use of A and heirs but if A marries B then to the use of C and heirs", A would get an equitable fee simple with a gift over of an equitable shifting executory interest in C. The grant to C is contingent on A marrying B, so it is sometimes called a "contingent equitable remainder", but the term remainder is properly used only for interests created in common law grants. C's interest cannot be a remainder because a remainder after a fee simple is void. If A's fee simple were a legal estate, we would have to decide whether it is a fee simple determinable or a fee simple subject to condition subsequent. Since with equitable estates we do not have to worry about the legal remainder rules that follow from those distinctions, we can say simply that A's fee simple is subject to an executory limitation — the shifting of the estate to C if A marries B.

Similarly, where O, prior to 1536, conveyed by livery of seisin the legal estate to A and his heirs to be effective when A married B, A would get nothing, for without any supporting prior particular estate, the freehold would have to spring from O to A when A married B, something that the legal remainder rules forbade. But if O raised a use with a transfer "to X and heirs for the use of A and heirs when A married B", O could avoid any problems of gaps in seisin. X would be seised of the fee simple, to hold for the use of O while waiting for A to marry, and thereafter for the use of A in fee simple. O would have an equitable fee simple subject to an equitable springing executory interest in fee simple in A — A's interest being conditional on marrying B.

Note the use of the word "executory" in identifying the contingent shifting and springing interests created in these examples. In this context, "executory interest" means that the interest has not yet and may never vest. Note as well that X, the feoffee to uses, does not get the equitable estate while waiting for A to marry B. Feoffees to uses are given the property to hold for the benefit of another person and so cannot take the benefit for themselves. While waiting for the named grantee of the equitable interest to meet the conditions specified in the grant, X holds the legal title for the benefit of the grantor by way of a resulting use. In any situation where there is no express use, the equitable title results back to O or O's estate. Thus, if O makes any conveyance of a fee simple to uses for a use that is less than a fee simple, the feoffee to uses holds legal title for the benefit of the *cestui que usent* for the duration of their estates, and then on a resulting use for the benefit of O or O's estate in fee simple. Thus, in a grant "to D and heirs for the use of A for life" prior to the *Statute of Uses*, D has a legal fee simple, A has a present equitable life estate, and O has a vested equitable reversion in fee simple.

What is the effect of the *Statute of Uses* on executory interests and resulting trusts? If you understand the mechanical method by which the Statute operates, you will understand what happens to these interests after 1536. Where a use has been raised either by livery of seisin, as in the examples used above, or where it is done by the bargain and sale deed, or perhaps even in a small number of cases by covenants to stand seised, the Statute executes the use. Therefore, where O conveyed to "D and heirs for the use of A and heirs but if A marries B then to the use of C and heirs", for a split second D has a legal fee simple, and A an equitable fee simple subject to C's equitable shifting executory interest in fee. The Statute then executes, D disappears, and A has a legal fee simple subject to a legal shifting executory interest in fee simple in C. Similarly, in the transfer from O "to D and heirs for the use of A and heirs when A marries B", the Statute takes D's legal fee simple and gives it to O, who thus has a legal fee simple subject to A's legal springing executory interest in fee simple.

But how can we have legal shifting and springing interests despite the legal remainder rules? Because, when the Statute turns the equitable interests into legal interests, they are not common law remainders, but legal executory interests created by the operation of the *Statute of Uses*. And the *Statute of Uses* said that *cestui que usent* were to be seised of the same estate in law that they had in equity. Moreover, since purely equitable interests were not subject to the legal remainder rules, judges held that legal executory interests were exempt, too — with one exception that we will discuss soon. Henceforth, by raising a use that was executed by the *Statute of Uses*, conveyancers could create legal future interests that were not possible with common law conveyances.

And remember that by using a form of conveyance that blocked or exhausted the Statute, conveyancers could still create purely equitable interests not subject to the *Statute of Uses* at all. After 1536, then, it was possible to create three kinds of contingent future interests: legal remainders, equitable executory interests and legal executory interests. But be careful. Not all jurisdictions are uniform in their treatment of these possibilities. Nearly every common law jurisdiction, following the English precedent of 1540, now has wills legislation, whereby no use need be raised to create springing and shifting executory devises. In *inter vivos* transfers, however, one generally has to raise a use in order to bring in the *Statute of Uses* and create springing and shifting freeholds.

## THE RULE IN *PUREFOY v. ROGERS*

If you have been following thus far, you should be wondering why we bother to distinguish between equitable executory interests and legal executory interests, since the legal remainder rules apply to neither. Indeed, you may be wondering why we even bothered to learn the rules. The answer to the second question is simple — we still have purely legal estates, created by grants that do not contain any uses, and these remain subject to the legal remainder rules. And to the first question — it is important to distinguish between legal and equitable executory interests because there is an exception to the rule that the legal remainder rules do not apply to legal executory interests. That exception is known as the Rule in *Purefoy v. Rogers* (1671), 85 E.R. 1181.

If you review the technical rules that so complicated conveyancing at common law, you will find that three stand out: the rule prohibiting conditions in strangers — no shifting freeholds; the rule prohibiting abeyance of seisin — no springing interests; and the destruction of contingent remainders that did not vest during or at the end of the prior particular estate. We have just seen that we can create shifting and springing interests in spite of the first two of these rules, either by granting an estate that is purely equitable or by raising a use that is executed by the *Statute of Uses* so as to create a legal executory interest. The Rule in *Purefoy v. Rogers* deals with the third rule.

Remember one of our early examples, in which O conveyed "to A for life, remainder to B and heirs if B is 21 at A's death". Prior to 1536, the state of the title at the effective date of the grant was a present life estate in A, and a contingent remainder in fee simple in B with a possible reversion in fee simple in O. If B reached the age of 21 during A's lifetime, B's estate vested in interest and then vested in possession when A died. But if B was, say, only 19 when A died, then B got nothing and O got the fee simple.

But now we know that we may be able to avoid this result by raising a use: if B is granted an equitable executory interest in fee, but is only 19 on A's death, the reversion puts the fee back in O, but only until B is ready to receive it, at 21. This is indeed what happens if O uses a form of conveyance that blocks or exhausts the *Statute of Uses*. O would then have an equitable fee simple subject to a springing executory interest in fee simple in B to take effect when B is 21. But if O uses a conveyance to uses that is executed by the *Statute of Uses* — with B receiving a legal rather than an equitable executory interest — the Rule in *Purefoy v. Rogers* says that if the executory interest can comply with the legal remainder rules, it must. Put differently: where a legal executory interest can comply with the legal remainder rules, it fails if it does not. Thus, where the condition for vesting in interest of a legal executory interest was one that could be met within the prior particular estate — a wait-and-see situation with a legal remainder — the Rule in *Purefoy v. Rogers* applied the wait-and-see rule to the legal executory interest, too. The legal executory interest would be void unless it vested in interest during or at the end of the prior particular estate. In the example above, a grant to B of a legal executory interest would fail if B were not 21 when A died.

But here as elsewhere, the fertile minds of conveyancers developed ways around obstacles. The Rule in *Purefoy v. Rogers* applies only to legal executory interests that were capable of complying with the legal remainder rules. It will not apply, therefore, to legal executory interests that, as legal remainders, would be void *ab initio*, because, for example, they can vest in interest only after some built-in gap in seisin following the end of the prior particular estate. The Rule in *Purefoy v. Rogers* applies only if there is a possibility that the legal executory interest might vest within the allowed period and in the allowed way. If it is clear from the outset that the legal executory interest could never comply with the legal remainders rules, it need not.

Therefore, to avoid *Purefoy v. Rogers*, O could provide for a gap between the prior particular estate and the vesting in interest of the legal executory interest, or leave out the supporting prior particular estate entirely. For example, O can avoid destruction of a legal executory interest by a conveyance "to X and heirs to the use of A for life, and one day following A's death to the use of B and heirs if B is 21 or so soon thereafter as B turns 21". There is nothing here to block or exhaust the *Statute of Uses*, so X disappears from the picture, A gets a legal life estate, and B gets a legal executory interest, to vest in interest on reaching the age of 21, but with vesting in possession to wait in any case until one day after the end of A's life estate. Since this grant would have been void *ab initio* as a contingent remainder, *Purefoy v. Rogers* does not apply. If B is not 21 when A dies, O gets the fee simple in reversion until B turns 21, when it springs back to B.

## EXECUTORY INTERESTS AND THE CLASS CLOSING RULES

Recall that a conveyance of a legal remainder to a class, "the children of A", for example, creates a contingent remainder for any children not yet born. Remainders "to grandchildren who reach the age of 21", or "winners of the Governor-General's Awards for Fiction for the next 15 years" are other examples of contingent remainders to a class. With such grants at common law, the class closes at the end of the prior particular estate, regardless of whether all possible parents have died and grandchildren have died young or reached the age of 21, or if the prior particular estate ends before the end of the 15 years. With legal remainders, the interests of people who meet the conditions during the prior particular estate vest in interest when the condition is met; if their interest has not vested at the death of the life tenant, the class closes and they are excluded. But with executory interests, whether legal or equitable, the class stays open until there is no possibility of other grantees meeting the condition. In a grant "to A for life, remainder to A's children and heirs", the result is the same whether one is dealing with a legal remainder or an executory interest, for A's death (plus the gestation period, if relevant) marks the end both of the wait-and-see period and the possibility of A producing children. But with executory interests that are contingent on reaching a certain age or meeting some other condition, the class stays open, even if the wait-and-see period extends beyond the prior particular estate. The interests of those who meet the condition vest when the condition is met, but remain subject to partial divestment as others meet the condition and claim a share.

## EQUITABLE ESTATES AND THE RULE IN *SHELLEY'S CASE*

There is one more technical common law rule that we can evade by a skilful combination of legal and equitable estates. Recall that one of the requirements for the application of the Rule in *Shelley's Case* (1581), 1 Co. Rep. 93b, is that the life estate to the ancestor and the attempted remainder to the whole line of succession must be both legal or both equitable. Thus, in the examples that we considered in Chapter Two, the Rule applied because we were dealing only with common law grants creating purely legal estates. The Rule will apply as well to a conveyance to uses that is not executed by the *Statute of Uses*, so that legal title remains with the feoffee to uses and both the life estate to the ancestor and the attempted remainder to the heirs are equitable estates. So, too, the Rule will apply if the Statute executes all of the uses, and converts the life estate and the remainder to legal interests.

Thus, if O conveyed "to T and heirs to maintain the property and pay the income to A for life with the income to go to A's heirs upon A's death", the grants to A and A's heirs are both equitable. T, a feoffee to uses with active duties, will have a legal fee simple only (the *Statute of Uses* does not execute conveyances to the use where the feoffee to uses has active duties); A will have an equitable life estate and an equitable fee simple in remainder; and, there being no intervening particular estates, A ends up with the present equitable fee simple by the doctrine of merger.

But if O devised "to T and heirs to maintain the property and pay the profits to A for life and, on A's death to convey the legal title to A's heirs for their use absolutely", A has an equitable estate but the heirs have a legal estate. So the Rule in *Shelley's Case* does not apply. A gets an equitable life estate and A's heirs get a legal fee simple in remainder (remember that the magic words of limitation are not necessary to create a fee simple in a will).

# THE MODERN TRUST

The combination of conveyances to uses and the *Statute of Uses*, as interpreted at common law and in equity, gives conveyancers choice and flexibility within a system based on rigid categories and highly technical rules. By adding a few words to our conveyances we can prevent the re-uniting of legal and equitable title that was the purpose of the Statute. It is thus still possible to create equitable estates — indeed, the *Statute of Uses* allowed conveyances to uses to flourish. But some things have changed. With feoffment by livery of seisin no longer necessary to transfer legal title, we are more likely to speak of a "trustee" than a feoffee to uses. And instead of *cestui que use*, we speak of the *cestui que trust* or the "beneficiary of the trust". And we generally speak of "trusts" rather than "uses". But the different terms do not have different meanings and can be used interchangeably.

So far we have looked at two kinds of trusts: those created expressly by the grantor, through a conveyance to uses or a bargain and sale, and those trusts that result to the grantor or the grantor's estate when the grant does not identify a beneficiary of the trust. Trusts created expressly by the grantor are called "express trusts" and trusts that result to the grantor, as we have seen, are called "resulting trusts". Both arise from the intentions of the grantor, express or, in the case of the resulting trust, implied. The constructive trust, considered in more detail below, is imposed by the courts at the request of the beneficiary of the trust, over the objections of the person who is ordered to hold property as a trustee, to prevent or punish unconscionable conduct.

## Express Trusts

An owner of property who intends to create an express trust with respect to that property may do so in writing, orally, or even by conduct. The owner may declare that henceforth he or she holds the property as a trustee for the beneficiary of the trust. An oral declaration of trust creates an enforceable trust, unless the subject matter of the trust is such that the *Statute of Frauds* requires that the trust be in writing, or evidenced in writing. Usually, however, the owner transfers the property to someone else, to hold on certain trusts, with the terms of the trust recorded in a Deed of Trust or Trust Settlement, identifying the subject matter of the trust, the trustee or trustees and their obligations, and the rights of the beneficiaries of the trust. Trusts legislation in the provinces and territories defines some of the powers and duties of trustees, and provides for both trustees and beneficiaries to apply to the court for various remedies if difficulties arise in interpreting the trust document or administering the trust.

Just as in mediaeval times, people create trusts in order to obtain the advantages of dividing the rights and obligations of ownership between a trustee or group of trustees and the beneficiaries of the trust. Trusts are still used to create property interests that would not be valid interests at common law. Trusts can also be used, as in mediaeval times, to acquire property without making the acquisition a matter of public record, as, for example, when a developer works through third parties to assemble the land needed for a major project. The trust can also be used to reduce one's tax liability, thereby permitting property owners to maximize the benefits and minimize the obligations of property ownership.

Property owners still turn to the trust when they want to make provision for relatives or charities, and to control the disposition of their assets on death. Testators may use a trust to create successive interests in the same property, giving, for example, a life interest to the surviving spouse and the remainder to children. In setting the terms of the trust, the testator can determine the appropriate balance between the rights of the spouse and children, rather than leaving that to the peculiar workings of the doctrine of waste. Parents also use *inter vivos* or testamentary trusts to provide for children who are under the age of majority, or who are adults but, because of some disability, are likely to need financial support and help with managing their finances. Trusts that give the trustee considerable discretion in how to use trust funds for the benefit of a disabled adult may ensure that money is there for the trust beneficiary when needed, without making him or her ineligible for government support programs.

In many of the grants used as examples in the text or the problems, the grantee's interest in the property depends on the grantee attaining a specified age. Courts may interpret these provisions as creating a condition precedent for the interest to vest in interest, or they may interpret the interest as vesting in interest at the effective date of the grant, with possession or enjoyment of the property postponed until the grantee reaches the specified age. In the latter case, with an interest in a trust, the rule in *Saunders v. Vautier* (1841), 49 E.R. 282, affd [1835-41] All E.R. Rep. 58 (L.C.) allows the beneficiary or beneficiaries to terminate the trust prematurely, that is, before reaching the specified age, provided that all the beneficiaries are ascertained, all have reached the age of majority, all have full mental capacity, and all join in asking the trustees to terminate the trust and transfer the trust property to the beneficiaries.

For example, if a testator leaves property to trustees on trust for her children until the youngest has reached the age of 35, and there are no gifts to others if a child dies before 35, the children can terminate the trust and obtain the property when the youngest reaches the age of majority. It is possible to avoid this result by expressing the age requirement as a condition for obtaining the interest, or by providing for an alternative beneficiary until the principal beneficiary or beneficiaries reach the specified age. Otherwise, in those jurisdictions that have not enacted legislation to abolish the rule in *Saunders v. Vautier*, beneficiaries can invoke the rule to defeat the intentions of the person creating the trust.

## Resulting Trusts

Resulting trusts, too, have their modern uses, but given their nature, often in *post facto* arguments about the meanings and consequences of people's actions. If a trust lacks an express provision naming a beneficiary, equity presumed that the trustee was intended to hold the title for the benefit of the creator of the trust. This conclusion follows from the common law presumption that rational economic actors do not transfer their property to someone without getting something in return, *i.e.*, rational people do not make gifts. If O transfers the title to property to A, the common law presumption is that O did not intend to give A beneficial ownership of the property but intended A to hold the property for the benefit of O. Similarly, a presumption of resulting trust arises where a person provides the purchase price for property but puts title in another's name.

Before statutory reform, the presumption of resulting trust applied to transactions in which a wife bought property and put it in her husband's name. In the converse situation, though, where a husband bought property and put it in his wife's name, the presumption of advancement, or gift, applied. Most Canadian common law jurisdictions have abolished the presumption between spouses, and substituted the presumption of resulting trust, or made application of the presumption of advancement gender-neutral. In *Pecore v. Pecore*, [2007] S.C.J. No. 17, [2007] 1 S.C.R. 795 (S.C.C.), the Surpeme Court ruled that the presumption of advancement applies to transfers of property from either parent to a minor child, but not to a transfer from a parent to an adult child, even if the adult remains dependent on the parent.

The presumption of resulting trust is rebuttable by evidence showing that the parties intended to transfer both the legal and beneficial title. This intention is shown by using the formulaic "for his/her/their own use absolutely" following the words of limitation in the document used to transfer title.

## Constructive Trusts

Constructive trusts are imposed as a remedy and do not require evidence, actual or presumed, of an intention to create a trust. There are two main kinds of constructive trusts recognized in Canadian law. Recall the discussion earlier in this chapter of the willingness of the Chancellor to hold the vendor of an estate in land accountable to the purchaser as a trustee of the title once the purchaser had paid the purchase price. The trust so created is an institutional constructive trust, and arises so long as a court of equity would grant the remedy of specific performance of the contract of purchase and sale. More generally, the institutional constructive trust is imposed in circumstances in which a person has acquired property for his or her own benefit, at the expense of another to whom the person owes a fiduciary duty, that is, an obligation to act toward the other with the utmost good faith. The other main kind of constructive trust, which is sometimes called the remedial constructive trust, is imposed in situations where, without imposition of the trust obligation, the person holding title to property would be unjustly enriched at the expense of someone who has contributed to the acquisition or improvement of that property.

The institutional constructive trust can be used in situations where a person wrongfully acquires property, even though that person obtained no financial benefit from doing so. For example, in *Soulos v. Korkontzilas*, [1997] S.C.J. No. 52, [1997] 2 S.C.R. 217 (S.C.C.), which explored the basis for the institutional constructive trust, a client sued a real estate agent who purchased a property for himself while supposedly negotiating for the property on behalf of the client. By the time of the trial, the market value of the property had fallen below the price paid by the real estate agent, but the client still wanted the property. The Supreme Court ruled that the real estate agent held the property on a constructive trust for the client, with the obligation to transfer the property to the client when the client paid the purchase price to the agent. Imposition of the trust obligation was necessary, the Court ruled, in order to return the parties to the position they would have been in had the real estate agent not breached his fiduciary duty, and to ensure that real estate agents and others in positions of trust and confidence remain faithful to their duty of loyalty.

The second type of constructive trust, the remedial constructive trust, has been used most commonly in Canada in the context of disputes about entitlement to property acquired during the course of an intimate relationship, when only one of the partners holds title to the property. As we will see in Chapter Twelve, since the late 1970s, the property rights of legally married couples are generally determined by provincial legislation mandating the equal sharing of defined categories of property, regardless of which spouse holds title to the property. Partners whose relationships are not governed by family property legislation, and who have not insisted on shared title to family property, may turn to the remedial constructive trust to establish rights to beneficial ownership of property acquired during the relationship. The constructive trust is available as a remedy to prevent unjust enrichment in other disputes, too, such as when benefits have been conferred under mistakes of fact or law, under compulsion, or as a result of ineffective transactions. Nonetheless, the facts necessary to establish a constructive trust arise most commonly in non-business settings, where the claimants may not have attended to protecting their legal position.

Initially, non-title holding partners in an intimate relationship tried to fit their claims within the existing resulting trust doctrine, arguing that their contributions to property made them owners in equity. As courts struggled to prevent one partner to an intimate relationship from leaving with all of the property accumulated during the relationship, they developed the idea of a resulting trust based on the "common intention" of the parties that the title-holding partner held title for the benefit of both partners. A resulting trust based solely on intention, however, without a transfer of property from the would-be beneficiary to the alleged trustee, is doctrinally unsound.

Faced with the doctrinal and practical limitations of the resulting trust, parties and courts found an alternative argument in the doctrine of unjust enrichment. To succeed with an unjust enrichment claim, the claimant must show that the defendant has been enriched by receiving a benefit from the claimant, that the claimant suffered a corresponding detriment in conferring the benefit, and there is no "juristic reason" for the enrichment. Juristic reasons to deny recovery may be that the claimant intended to make a gift of the benefit, or was obliged to confer the benefit by law or because of a contractual commitment. The ordinary remedy for unjust enrichment is an order for monetary compensation, but in Pettkus v Becker, [1980] S.C.J. No. 103, [1980] 2 S.C.R. 834 (S.C.C.), the Supreme Court held that where the claimant can demonstrate a link or causal connection between the benefit conferred and the acquisition, preservation, maintenance or improvement of the disputed property, the title holder may be declared to be a trustee holding a share of the property proportionate to the unjust enrichment on a constructive trust for the benefit of the claimant.

Despite a series of decisions in which the Supreme Court used the constructive trust as a mechanism for adjusting property entitlements between intimate partners, lawyers were reluctant to abandon alternative claims based on a "common intention" resulting trust. In 2011, the Supreme Court stated, in a unanimous decision in Kerr v. Baranow, [2011] S.C.J. No. 10 at para. 29, [2011] 1 S.C.R. 269 (S.C.C.), that the resulting trust arising solely from the common intention of the parties "no longer has a useful role to play in resolving property and financial disputes in domestic cases". Instead, claims based on contributions from a non-title holding partner should be framed as claims of unjust enrichment, so that the court could consider the "equities of the particular case . . . transparently and according to principle, rather than masquerading behind often artificial attempts to find common intent to support what the court thinks for unstated reasons is a just result" (at para. 28).

Unlike family property legislation, which generally mandates an equal division of most property accumulated by the spouses during the marriage, courts can apply the doctrine of unjust enrichment flexibly. When parties have worked together in what the Supreme Court identified in Kerr v. Baranow as a "joint family venture", each is entitled to a share in the proceeds of the venture that is proportionate to their contribution. The contribution can be direct or indirect. A partner who pays the household expenses or assumes primary responsibility for household maintenance or child care and thus contributes to the other's ability to acquire property is entitled to a share in that property at the end of the relationship. Where a monetary award would be inadequate, the court can order the title holder to hold property in whole or in part on a constructive trust for the benefit of the other partner.

The constructive trust is a flexible remedy and Canadian courts have been willing to adapt it to a variety of situations. Doubtless lawyers will find occasions to argue for its further development and broader deployment.

# 10

# THE RULE AGAINST PERPETUITIES

The legal remainder rules, although developed primarily to prevent gaps in seisin or shifts in seisin, served to limit the length of time one would wait to see whether a contingent remainder would vest. If a condition precedent for taking a grant was not satisfied during the lifetime of the holder of the prior life estate, then the potential grantee lost out on the grant. But when the court of equity granted recognition to equitable executory interests that did not involve any question of seisin, and so were exempt from the legal remainder rules, landowners obtained the ability to create contingent interests that need not vest within or at the moment of termination of the prior particular estate. And when operation of the *Statute of Uses, 1535* (U.K.), 27 Hen. 8, c. 10, created legal executory interests, they too, subject to the Rule in *Purefoy v. Rogers*, (1671), 85 E.R. 1181, were exempt from the legal remainder rules. Thus, after 1536, there were few limits on the possibilities for tying up land with contingencies that might not vest until far into the future. Conveyancers took advantage of the new executory interests to impose conditions on vesting and on transfers that would keep land in the family. In consequence, landowners could not readily use their land to generate capital for land improvements or entrepreneurial ventures. In order to set new limits on the time within which contingent interests might vest, the courts developed, by a rather circuitous route that need not concern us here, a rule against remoteness of vesting, which came to be called the Rule Against Perpetuities.

## THE RULE IN *WHITBY v. MITCHELL*

In the process of limiting contingent interests, courts developed the Rule in *Whitby v. Mitchell* (1890), 44 Ch. D. 85 (C.A.), to deal with grants to unborn grantees. Suppose O wants the property amassed in his lifetime to remain in his family, but he knows that conveyancers, with the collusion of the courts, have circumvented the fee tail. O then conveys "to my son for life, with remainder to my son's son for life and further remainder to my son's son's children and their heirs", thus determining who owns the property for a very long time.

The Rule in *Whitby v. Mitchell* prevents this attempt to control from beyond the grave by declaring void any attempt to give a remainder to the issue of an unborn grantee. Thus, if at the date of the following grant from O "to A for life, then to A's first son for life, remainder to that son's children and heirs", A had no son, then A received a life estate, his potential first son a contingent remainder for life, and the further remainder to the grandchildren was void. The Rule in *Whitby v. Mitchell* was abolished in England in the property law reforms of 1925, but not in all Canadian jurisdictions. Its effect is often duplicated by the more far-reaching Rule against Perpetuities.

## STATEMENT OF THE RULE AGAINST PERPETUITIES

The Rule Against Perpetuities has been stated thus: a future interest is void unless it would vest in interest, if at all, only within a period measured by lives in being plus a further period of 21 years. The Rule against Perpetuities applies to legal remainders and executory interests, both legal and equitable. The common law rule, unmodified by statute, is concerned with what might happen, not what actually happens. If there is any possibility of a contingent interest vesting in interest beyond the perpetuity period, the grant of that interest is void *ab initio*. We do not wait to see whether, as events transpire, the interest would have vested within the permitted period.

Because the perpetuity period is measured by the lives of particular individuals plus 21 years, it does not have a fixed length, but varies from grant to grant. Indeed, even the 21 years can be extended by the period of gestation, so that a child *en ventre sa mere* can be a life in being. If there are no relevant lives in being, the perpetuity period is 21 years.

## LIVES IN BEING

How do we identify the relevant lives in being? First, lives in being, as the term suggests, are human beings who are alive at the effective date of the grant. However, not everyone who is alive at that moment will qualify as a life in being. Think about the role that lives in being play in the Rule Against Perpetuities — to determine the length of time beyond which vesting is impermissible. In order to calculate that length of time, we need to be able to identify the lives in being with certainty, and keep track of them, so we need a group that is smaller than everyone who is alive at the effective date of the grant.

It is possible for the grantor to define the time permitted for vesting by naming explicit lives in being, and setting the time limit for vesting as their lives plus 21 years. If these lives are ascertainable, such a grant is valid. These clauses protect the grant from the Rule against Perpetuities by setting an explicit period for vesting that is within the period permitted by the Rule, and cutting off the possibility of vesting beyond that period.

Older grants sometimes used a "royal lives clause" for this purpose, stating that the interest of the potential grantee would be valid only if it vested within 21 years of the death of the last surviving direct descendant of Queen Victoria who was living at the effective date of the grant. Given that Queen Victoria had many children and grandchildren, such a clause would provide a long period for vesting, barring some calamity that afflicted the entire royal family. And given the prominence of the family, at least in the 19th century, the grant was not likely to be declared void for uncertainty because of the difficulties of determining the date of death of the last of the group to die. Today, though, if one wanted to create a long, but permissible, period for interests to vest, it would be safer to name as explicit lives in being the direct descendants of the current monarch who are alive at the effective date of the grant.

Without explicitly named lives in being, the period for vesting will be the lives of any implicit lives in being, plus 21 years. Implicit lives in being are people who have a relevant biological relationship to the potential grantees of contingent interests or to the conditions for their interest to vest. Thus, implicit lives in being are people whose lives, or deaths, determine who is eligible to receive a contingent interest or when a contingent interest will vest. For example, if O grants Blackacre "unto and to the use of Trust T on trust for A for life, then on trust in fee simple for the children of B who attain the age of 25", B is an implicit life in being. Even though B receives nothing in the grant, it is B's death that ends the possibility of potential grantees joining the class.

Suppose that at the effective date of this grant, B has three living children, Dick, Jane and Sally. Even though they are alive, they do not count as implicit lives in being because the grant is not to them but to a group of which they are members. This group could grow to include members born after the effective date of the grant, because B could have more children. Because of the possibility that B might have children born after the effective date of the grant who might meet the conditions for their interest to vest more than 21 years after the death of A and B, the grant to the children, including the living children, would be void under the common law Rule. A grant on trust for Dick, Jane, and Sally when they reach the age of 25 would not be void, because the potential grantees are now people who are alive at the effective date of the grant, and the condition for vesting is one that they can meet, if at all, only within their own lifetimes. In some jurisdictions, reform legislation would interpret a grant such as the first one above as not including any children born after the effective date of the grant, in order to achieve at least some of the grantor's intentions.

## THE REQUIREMENT FOR CERTAINTY

How does the Rule Against Perpetuities work? First, notice that it deals with vesting. If we have an estate that is already vested in interest, the Rule has no application, regardless how far into the future the estate will vest in possession. The Rule applies only to contingent remainders or executory interests subject to a condition precedent. Thus, when O grants a determinable estate and retains a possibility of reverter, the Rule Against Perpetuities cannot apply, for, from the beginning, a possibility of reverter is a vested interest. Contrast this with the fee simple subject to condition subsequent, in which O gives A a fee simple and then provides for the possibility of regaining the fee through exercising the right of re-entry for condition broken. Because the breach of the condition subsequent is a condition precedent for the exercise of the right or re-entry, if the event that breaches the condition might occur beyond the perpetuity period, then the condition is void from the beginning and A gets a fee simple absolute. The difference is hard to justify on policy grounds; failing to appreciate it can defeat the grantor's or testator's intentions. In some jurisdictions, legislators have intervened to assimilate the two estates into one, or to have the Rule Against Perpetuities apply to both of them.

Note that it is not enough that the contingent interest actually vest within the perpetuity period. For a grant to escape the common law Rule Against Perpetuities, we must be certain from the beginning, that is, from the effective date of the grant, that there is no possibility, however unlikely or remote, that the conditions for an interest to vest in interest might be met, if at all, beyond the perpetuity period. It follows, then, that we cannot wait to see what actually happens or take into account what we know has happened: we must decide the grant's validity taking into account all possibilities. With an *inter vivos* conveyance, we must determine, at the date of delivery of the deed to the potential grantee, that the condition can only be met, if at all, before the death of the lives in being plus 21 years. Similarly with a testamentary disposition, we must make this determination on the testator's death.

Consider a grant "to the woman who stands highest in this year's graduating class from the Faculty of Law if she becomes Chief Justice of Canada". Here, the grant is to one of a group of people who are now living (despite what their professors might think some mornings), and the condition is one that can be met by that person, if at all, only during her lifetime. As there is no possibility that this interest can vest beyond the perpetuity period, the Rule Against Perpetuities has no application. We can wait and see if the top woman graduate meets the condition of becoming Chief Justice.

Now consider a grant "to the first woman from Prince Edward Island to become Chief Justice of Canada". Here we have not limited the possible takers of this grant to persons now living and, since it is possible that the first woman from Prince Edward Island to become Chief Justice might not yet be born, and that her appointment might come well beyond the perpetuity period, the grant is void *ab initio*. The Rule does not let us wait and see. But, assuming no question of uncertainty as to what it means to be from Prince Edward Island, we can save this grant by adding further conditions that limit the time for vesting to a time within the perpetuity period. For example, we can define the potential grantee as "the first woman from Prince Edward Island now living to become Chief Justice of Canada". As in the first example, we now have a condition that can be met, if at all, only within the lifetime of a life in being. It is possible that no person from Prince Edward Island now living will meet the qualifying conditions, but we can wait and see.

What is important is certainty, and certainty depends both on the wording of the conveyance and on the facts of the situation. Suppose O devises an equitable estate (equitable so that contingent interests need not vest during the prior particular estate) to A's daughters for life, and then to A's grandchildren and heirs who have an article published in *Canadian Forum* before reaching the age of 21. If A is dead at O's death, the effective date of the conveyance, we do not have to worry about the Rule against Perpetuities at all. Since A cannot produce more daughters to share in the life estate, all of the possible holders of the life estate — all the daughters that A can ever have — are alive at the effective date of the grant and are therefore lives in being. Since A cannot have any more children, his children are relevant lives in being, and his grandchildren, if any, who meet the condition cannot do so more than 21 years after their own birth, which cannot be more than 21 years (plus the gestation period, if relevant) after the death of their parent. So the condition for vesting will be met, if at all, within 21 years of the death of a life in being.

But if A is alive the devise to the grandchildren is void for a grandchild who meets the condition might be the child of a child of A who was born after the effective date of the grant. The condition is still one that can be met only within 21 years of the death of the parent, but since — A being alive — A's children are not lives in being, 21 years after the death of a parent might be more than 21 years after the death of all relevant lives in being.

Now change the devise a little. Leave out the condition that the article must be published before the grandchild is 21. Now the devise to the grandchildren is void even if A is dead when O dies. A's children are lives in being (since A is dead and cannot have any more). But the grandchildren are not lives in being unless all of A's children are dead, too.

Because of the possibility that a grandchild born after the effective date of the grant might have an article published in the *Canadian Forum*, and because this might not happen until after A's children have died, the grant to the grandchildren is void *ab initio* unless A and A's children have predeceased the testator, making the grandchildren lives in being.

## COMMON TRAPS

Look again at the previous devise. Suppose now that when O dies, A is alive but well past the age at which a person is ordinarily fertile. This would not change anything for the Rule requires absolute, not statistical, certainty. Even if A were an elderly widow at the effective date of the grant, the contingent interest would be void because the common law assumes fertility from the moment of birth to the moment of death. Rather than waiting to see if A has more children, the Rule acts on the remote possibility of A conceiving, and voids the contingent interest *ab initio*. Though it might seem sensible to limit our consideration to real possibilities (ignoring the new reproductive technologies, as the common law so far has), the common law rule favours legal certainty over scientific prediction — hence, the "fertile octogenarian" and the "precocious toddler", considered by the common law to be capable of reproducing from the moment of birth until death.

A similar problem arises with a grant of a remainder to children or grandchildren with a contingency that can be met during or at the end of a prior life estate that is granted to an "unborn widow". Consider a grant "to A for life, then to A's widow for life, then to A's children then living in fee simple". Note that the words "then living" make this a contingent remainder — contingent on the grantees being alive at the end of the prior particular estate. The drafter of this grant, thinking of A and his lovely wife, did not consider the possibility that something might happen and A might marry again, and that his second wife might be a woman who was not born at the date of the grant and therefore not herself a life in being. Since A could also have more children after the date of the grant, one of these, again not a life in being, could survive the widow and so meet the condition. But the widow's death, the date for vesting, could be more than 21 years after A's death — the death of the only relevant life in being. So the grant to A's children is void *ab initio*. We could save this grant by removing the condition of surviving the widow, so that the interest of the grantees vests in interest at birth, subject to partial divestment as others are born.

Another common trap for unwary practitioners is sometimes called "the magic gravel pit". Consider a devise "to my trustees to work the gravel pit until it is exhausted, and then to sell the land and divide the proceeds among my grandchildren then living". Everyone except the common law knows that the gravel pit will be exhausted within two years. But as the law takes into account the remote possibility that the land might not be sold within the perpetuity period, this grant is void. Note that if the grantees in this devise had been the testator's children, the grant would be valid. As the dead testator can have no more children, the children themselves are relevant lives in being, and the grant must vest, if at all, while they are alive. This kind of trap — failing to take account of remote possibilities — is also called "the evil probate clerk", from *Lucas v. Hamm*, 364 P.2d 685 (Cal. 1961), in which the California Supreme Court held that it was not professional negligence for a practitioner to fail to recognize that the Rule against Perpetuities invalidated a devise in which the interest in the grantees was to vest five years after the will was probated. Ordinarily, the probating process would be completed in a few months, but the common law takes account of the possibility of the process continuing beyond the perpetuity period.

Recall the discussion of oil and gas leases in Chapter Seven. It is common in the oil and gas industry for the fee simple owner of the petroleum rights to enter into a second lease, called a top lease, during the term of a first lease. The top lease is intended to take effect on the termination of the first lease, which may have a secondary term that is defined as continuing for as long as the leaseholder continues to produce the leased substances. If the top lease as drafted gives an immediate vested interest, with possession or enjoyment postponed until the end of the first lease, it will not violate the Rule Against Perpetuities. But if the top lease is worded so that it vests in interest only when the first leaseholder ceases to produce oil and gas from the leased property — an event that might not occur within the perpetuity period — the top lease will be void under the Rule Against Perpetuities. Drafters must choose their words carefully to avoid this outcome, and must be wary of copying precedent clauses from jurisdictions in which the Rule Against Perpetuities has been modified or abolished by legislation.

## GUARDING AGAINST THE RULE

It should be clear from the examples above that the application of the Rule Against Perpetuities depends on the nature of the grant and the possibilities existing at the effective date of the grant. You must consider the two together, as wording that will create a valid interest in some circumstances will create void interests in others. Ask yourself: does the grant create a contingent interest that might vest more than 21 years after the death of the relevant lives in being? If there is any possibility that the answer to this question is yes, then the Rule operates to invalidate the grant *ab initio* — we cannot wait and see whether vesting actually occurs within the perpetuity period. Remember that the Rule is also called the rule against remoteness of vesting — it is not concerned with the length of any intermediate estate, but with defining the outside limit within which a contingent interest might vest, and eliminating grants which have any possibility of vesting beyond this period.

Practitioners may protect grants from the Rule, as we have seen, by limiting the time for vesting to the perpetuity period. For example, a grant "to the first woman from Prince Edward Island to become Chief Justice of the Supreme Court of Canada, providing she does so within 21 years of the death of the Supreme Court justices now serving" is valid, because there are two conditions that the potential grantee must meet: to become Chief Justice of the Supreme Court and to do so within a time that is within the perpetuity period.

Practitioners may also use the legal remainder rules to create a wait-and-see period that will protect a grant from being void *ab initio* because of the Rule Against Perpetuities. A grant of a contingent interest subject to the legal remainder rules will comply with the Rule Against Perpetuities if the prior particular estate can be held only by a person who was alive at the effective date of the grant. Under the legal remainder rules, if the remainder does not vest in interest during or at the end of the prior particular estate, it fails — we wait no longer. Thus, if the prior particular estate is held by a life in being, the remainder must vest, if at all, within the perpetuity period. The time limit for vesting set by the legal remainder rules, if the holder of the prior particular estate is a life in being, is shorter than the perpetuity period.

As you know, the legal remainder rules do not apply to equitable executory interests, but it is possible to protect legal executory interests from the Rule Against Perpetuities by ensuring that the Rule in *Purefoy v. Rogers* applies to the grant. Recall that, according to *Purefoy v. Rogers*, if a legal executory interest can comply with the legal remainder rules, then it must comply: if there is a possibility that the legal executory interest could vest in interest within the prior particular estate, it must vest within that prior particular estate or fail. Although under this Rule there is no guarantee that the legal executory interest will be valid, the wait-and-see period is preserved, rather than the interest being struck down *ab initio*.

Look again at the earlier example of the conveyance "to A's daughters for life, and then to A's grandchildren and heirs who have an article published in *Canadian Forum*". But this time, make this a conveyance to uses that is executed by the *Statute of Uses*, so that the contingent interest is a legal executory interest rather than an equitable interest. Is it possible for the grant to the grandchildren to comply with the legal remainder rules? Yes, a grandchild could meet the condition during the prior particular estate. The Rule in *Purefoy v. Rogers* thus applies and the grant to the grandchildren will fail unless it vests before the death of the longest living of the daughters. Will this requirement save the grant to the grandchildren from being destroyed by the Rule against Perpetuities? Yes, if A is dead at the effective date of the grant. Then the only people who can take the prior particular estate are lives in being and, because of *Purefoy v. Rogers*, it is their lives, not the lives of the grandchildren, that set the time limit for meeting the condition. Of course, if A is still alive, it is possible for a child of A's to be born after the effective date of the grant, so that the prior particular estate need not be held by a life in being, and the interest to the grandchildren is void.

One more variation on this example: a conveyance "to X to the use of A's daughters, Ann, Mary and Esmeralda, for life, and then to A's grandchildren and heirs who have an article published in the *Canadian Forum*". Again, the interests created are legal executory interests, but this time the prior particular estate is given not to a class but to three named individuals who are lives in being. Because the legal executory interest could vest during the prior particular estate, *Purefoy v. Rogers* says that it is void unless it does so, and thus the grant to the grandchildren is protected from destruction by the Rule Against Perpetuities. We can wait and see if any grandchildren meet the condition during the lives of Ann, Mary and Esmeralda. If none do, then the grant fails at the termination of the life estates, and O or O's estate gets the fee simple in reversion. But at least we can wait and see.

## REFORM OR ABOLITION OF THE RULE

Jurisdictions that have provided legislative relief from the implacability of the Rule often do so by substituting a wait-and-see provision for the requirement that one determine at the outset, based on remote possibilities, whether conditions for vesting might be met beyond the permitted perpetuity period. Reforms may also apply realistic assumptions about when people are past the age of child-bearing. As well, given the difficulties of determining a permitted period when it is defined by relevant lives in being, reform legislation may provide the alternative of a fixed period. Despite the Rule's supposed focus on remoteness of vesting, this period may be quite long. British Columbia's legislation, the *Perpetuity Act*, R.S.B.C. 1996, c. 358, for example, validates all contingent interests which must vest in interest, if at all, within 80 years from the date of their creation. Grants that do not meet this criteria are not voided *ab initio*, but are presumed to be valid until actual events establish that the interest is incapable of vesting within the common law perpetuity period. The British Columbia *Perpetuity Act* also constrains some of the capriciousness of the Rule, with provisions for determining the relevant lives in being, and providing that, where there are no relevant lives in being, the perpetuity period is 80 years, rather than the 21 years of the common law Rule.

Piecemeal reform of the Rule Against Perpetuities may mitigate some of its harshness and eliminate some of the common traps, but it does not reduce its complexity or the likelihood of litigation over how the Rule applies in particular situations. Manitoba and Saskatchewan have abolished the Rule completely, with, it would seem, no loss of political or economic stability. In a report released in December 2010, the Law Reform Commission of Nova Scotia recommended abolition of the Rule, along with expansion of the courts' jurisdiction to vary the terms of existing trusts and of non-trust unvested interests: see *Final Report — The Rule Against Perpetuities* (Halifax, NS: Law Reform Commission of Nova Scotia, 2010).

In jurisdictions that have not yet abolished the Rule against Perpetuities, you can avoid trouble by drafting only conveyances that vest immediately rather than on the happening of some contingency. It may not always be possible or prudent to discourage your clients from imposing conditions in *inter vivos* grants or testamentary bequests and devises. Thus, when drafting interests subject to conditions, reduce the likelihood of forgetting about some remote possibility that might make the conveyance void because of the Rule Against Perpetuities by being as specific as possible. For example, use individual's names rather than generic terms such as widow, children and grandchildren. And in your spare time, lobby for legislation to abolish the Rule, or, if there is concern about a sudden resurgence of demand for conditions that would tie up property indefinitely, to replace the rule with a fixed and easily ascertainable wait-and-see period for vesting of contingent interests.

# 11

# CONCURRENT CO-OWNERSHIP

We have seen how the bundle of rights and obligations that makes up ownership can be divided into various estates and interests and that different people may have rights and obligations with respect to the same land at the same time. O may divide the circle of fee simple absolute by conveying, for example, a life estate to A and a remainder in fee simple to B, so that A and B have different estates in the same property at the same time. A has the immediate right to possession of the land, while B's right to possession is postponed until A's death. Or O could convey a leasehold while retaining the reversion in fee simple. The person who holds legal title may hold it on trust for a *cestui que trust*. There may be others who have rights based on licences, *profits à prendre*, easements or covenants. All of these are forms of shared ownership, but they are not the focus of this chapter. Here we consider the rights and obligations of people who share the same interest in the same land at the same time.

Up to now we have been concerned primarily with what is known as sole ownership of land, where O has conveyed A's estate to A alone. But what happens if O conveys the same estate to both A and B? What about a grant "to A and B and heirs". Now both have a fee simple estate, created at the same time, in the same land. As a co-owner, each has the right to possess the whole of the property. If it is a house, they do not each own half a house; they share an estate in fee simple in the property, giving each of them the equal right to possession of the whole. But what happens when A dies? Does B now own the whole property or will A's heirs, either those named in A's will or those who take on intestacy, step into A's place and share the house with B? The answer in any particular case will depend on the form of the grant and what has happened since.

Early English common law recognized four forms of co-ownership: joint tenancy, tenancy in common, tenancy by the entirety, and co-parcenary. Tenancy by the entirety disappeared along with the legal doctrine of marital unity, whereby at law husband and wife were one person, and that person was the husband. Co-parcenary is also obsolete. It arose by operation of law in situations where, there being no son, property that would have gone to him by primogeniture was shared instead by the daughters. Joint tenancy and tenancy in common remain alternatives which people must choose between when buying property together.

## JOINT TENANCIES AND TENANCIES IN COMMON

In the tenancy in common and the joint tenancy, all co-owners have an equal right to possession and use of the whole property, and, without a court order, no co-owner can exclude another from possession. Each co-owner, subject to legislation concerning spousal rights (to be discussed in Chapter Twelve), can make *inter vivos* dispositions of his or her share in the property, although there may be a limited market for a share of an undivided property. But only the tenant in common can dispose of his or her share of the property by will. Joint tenants, in contrast, are constrained by the right of survivorship. On the death of a joint tenant, his or her share of the property goes by the *jus accrescendi* to the surviving co-owners, with the longest living of them ending up as sole owner.

Whether a particular grant creates a joint tenancy or a tenancy in common depends, among other things, on the intention of the grantor. The intention to create a joint tenancy is best evidenced by using the words "as joint tenants" in the words of deed or feoffment. Common law presumed a joint tenancy if the Four Unities (described below) were present, unless there was something in the conveyance showing that the grantees should take as tenants in common. But equity favoured a tenancy in common. Gradually the common law courts reached the same result, interpreting almost any expression except "as joint tenants" as words of severance indicating an intention to create a tenancy in common. Words of severance include such phrases as "in equal shares", "share and share alike", "to be divided between", "to be distributed in joint and equal proportions", "equally", and "severally". When a particular grant contains a contradictory statement, such as "jointly in equal shares", the contradiction is resolved by giving more importance to the first word or phrase if a deed, but to the last if a will. Most jurisdictions have now reversed the common law presumption so that a conveyance to two or more grantees creates a tenancy in common unless the conveyance clearly shows the intention to create a joint tenancy. Where, however, property is conveyed to two or more co-owners as trustees or executors, the presumption is that they take title as joint tenants, since they were given the property not for themselves and their heirs but to carry out certain duties.

We know that different people may own the legal and the equitable interest in property. Similarly, co-owners may hold legal title in one form of co-ownership and equitable title in the other. For example, if A and B take title as joint tenants, but A has contributed all of the purchase price, then in equity B will hold his or her interest on a resulting trust for A, unless B can prove that in putting B's name on the title, A was making a gift to B of a half interest in the property. In most of the Canadian jurisdictions, family property legislation provides that where A and B are legally married, taking title to property as co-owners raises the presumption of the intention to share ownership equally, as joint tenants.

Whether co-owners hold as tenants in common or joint tenants is most likely to become an issue after one of the co-owners has died. The surviving co-owner(s) may claim to have acquired the deceased's share by the right of survivorship, while beneficiaries under the will or those entitled to take on intestacy may claim to have inherited the deceased's share. In each case, whether a joint tenancy was created initially and whether it still exists is a matter or fact. In some situations, the form of co-ownership may be important, even though the surviving co-owner will end up with the deceased co-owner's share, whether it is acquired by right of survivorship or by inheritance. The estate's tax liability, the size of the executor's fee, or rights of the deceased's surviving spouse may differ if the co-owned property does not pass through the estate, but goes directly to the surviving co-owner(s) by right of survivorship.

## The Four Unities

Intention by itself, however, is not enough to create a joint tenancy. The co-owners must also enjoy the four unities — possession, interest, time and title. All four must be present for a joint tenancy; if one of them is destroyed, the joint tenancy is severed and the co-ownership continues as a tenancy in common. The existence of the four unities is not proof that the co-owners hold title as joint tenants; all four unities may be present in a tenancy in common, too. The only unity that is required for a tenancy in common, however, is the unity of possession. Let us look at each of the unities in turn.

### *Unity of possession*

With unity of possession, each co-owner is entitled to possession of all of the property, subject to the equal right to possession of the other co-owners. If the grant to A and B specifies that A is to have the east half of the property and B the west half, and that neither is to go on the other's half, the grant has created neither a joint tenancy nor a tenancy in common since there is no shared ownership. Each grantee has been granted a separate parcel of land, with no unity of possession. (Such a grant might well be void if the grantor has not complied with the subdivision requirements of the relevant planning legislation, but that is another matter.) Note that unity of possession means only that each owner is entitled to equal possession of the undivided whole; choosing not to exercise the right to possession does not, by itself, destroy the unity of possession.

### *Unity of interest*

For unity of interest, each of the co-owners must have the same estate in the land, each must have an equal share in that estate, and each must have the same quality of estate — legal, equitable, or both. Suppose that A and B hold Blackacre as joint tenants in fee simple and A grants C a security interest in the property by way of a mortgage that transfers A's legal fee simple to C, leaving A with the equity of redemption. (Rarely would a creditor be so foolish as to take a mortgage from only one co-owner, but this is a hypothetical.) Since A no longer has the same estate as B, the joint tenancy is severed and the co-ownership converted to a tenancy in common. The unity of interest is also destroyed if one of the co-owners declares bankruptcy, since his or her property vests by operation of law in the trustee in bankruptcy. Similarly, if A sold a part of his or her interest to C, the joint tenancy would be severed, because B would still have a half interest in the fee simple, while A and C share a half interest. A and C could be joint tenants with respect to the interest they share, if they shared it equally, but they are tenants in common with B.

With a joint tenancy of a fee simple, we would expect that a grant by one of the co-owners of a life estate or leasehold would sever the joint tenancy, because the remaining co-owners have a present fee simple while the grantor has a fee simple in reversion. But some authorities say that the joint tenancy would only be suspended, and would revive if all of the co-owners were still alive at the termination of the life tenancy or the leasehold. If it is a life estate or a leasehold that is owned by the joint tenants, a grant by one of them of his or her interest will sever the joint tenancy, there being no reversion in the grantor.

### *Unity of time*

Unity of time means that all of the co-owners receive their estates at the same time; vesting in interest must take place simultaneously. We are not concerned here with what happens when O conveys a life estate to A and then a similar estate to B, for A and B are not concurrent co-owners. They have estates that vest in interest at the same time but they are different estates; B's will not vest in possession until A's ends. But where O has, by *inter vivos* grant, conveyed property "to C for life with a remainder to C's children and heirs when they reach the age of 21", the grant to the children must be as tenants in common, for although they have the same interest, it will vest in interest at different times, as each turns 21. Similarly, an *inter vivos* grant, "to A for life, remainder to the children of B and C and heirs who survive their father", must create a tenancy in common unless B and C die at exactly the same time, for the children's interests will vest only on their father's death. The result would be different if either of these grants had been made in a conveyance to uses or as a devise, for then the rule requiring simultaneous vesting would not apply.

### *Unity of title*

For unity of title, A and B must acquire their estates from the same instrument, whether a will or a deed, or, if their title is based on adverse possession, they must have taken possession of the land at the same time. It might appear at first glance that there is no substantial difference between "time" and "title". But consider the examples above. There, the grantees received their interests under the same instrument — O's deed — and thus satisfied the "title" requirements. But they did not meet the condition of unity of time. Unity of title can be destroyed even if the estates and shares of the co-owners do not change — by one of the co-owners, say A, signing and delivering a deed from A to A. Now A's title derives not from the original deed to all of the co-owners but from the second deed from A to A. A's action has severed the joint tenancy unilaterally and converted it into a tenancy in common, depriving all of the co-owners of the right of survivorship. They are still co-owners, owning the same shares as before, but now they can devise their shares by will, if they know of the change in title effected unilaterally by A. Some Canadian common law jurisdictions have enacted legislation to protect co-owners from unilateral severance of the joint tenancy.

## ENDING CO-OWNERSHIP

When joint tenants or tenants in common no longer wish to continue their shared ownership, they have several options. Where co-owners have a falling out and cannot agree on how to divide the property, they may apply under the relevant legislation for a court order partitioning the property or for its sale with a division of the proceeds. Partition or sale is a discretionary remedy, but the co-owner(s) who oppose it have the burden of establishing that partition would be unjust or unfeasible. Of course, applying for a court order is a last resort, when negotiations have failed. Co-owners do not need court intervention to sell their share to the other co-owner(s) or to someone else, or to sell the whole property and divide the proceeds.

## CONDOMINIUMS

The form of ownership that exists in most condominium developments combines individual ownership and shared ownership. Curiously, people who own a fee simple or an equity of redemption in their property talk about owning the tangible entity, such as the house or the cottage, while people who own an office, townhouse, apartment or other condominium property often talk of owning a condominium, as if that were the name of the tangible property rather than a term for a particular form of ownership.

In a condominium development, each owner owns a fee simple estate in part of the property individually or as a joint tenant or tenant in common with one or more co-owners. In addition, the owner(s) of each individual fee simple estate share with all owners of individual units as tenants in common ownership of common areas — driveways, parking lots, recreational facilities, lobbies, hallways, elevators, foundations, common walls and roofs. In a situation of shared ownership, there are many ways to provide for ongoing maintenance and expenses; in condominium developments, owners are commonly required, as a condition of purchasing their unit, to purchase a share in a condominium corporation that manages the development. The corporation by-laws may require unit owners to contribute to a contingency fund for maintaining the common areas.

The creation and title registration of condominium developments, a relatively recent addition to the possibilities of estate ownership, is governed by statute generally. Developed primarily as a way to spread risk, condominium ownership requires individual purchasers to finance a development project, with the advantage, not available to leaseholders, that they will benefit from any increase in the price of the property. As well, the condominium form of ownership can perform some of the functions of covenants, as discussed in Chapter Seven, without the same concern over enforceability by and against subsequent owners.

# 12

# FAMILY PROPERTY

As we have seen, the basic structure and concepts of property that developed in feudal England are still very much part of the law of the provinces and territories in common law Canada. The framework of family property law, however, is found in recent legislation. Although property rights of intimate partners are still determined primarily by the general property law, intimate partners by legislation have rights in each others' property on marriage breakdown, and, in some jurisdictions, on death of a spouse. In the context of marriage breakdown, support and property questions are usually dealt with under two separate legal regimes: the federal *Divorce Act*, R.S.C. 1985, c. 3 (2nd Supp.) provides for orders for support and child custody, while the applicable provincial or territorial legislation provides for orders for the division of family property.

If family property is real property on an Indian reserve, or on lands over which a First Nation has rights of self-government, provincial or territorial family law may have limited application. Disputes between intimate partners about their family property may raise conflict of laws questions, too. Under general conflict of laws principles, disputes about land, including disputes between intimate partners, have to be litigated where the land is, as courts do not have authority to make orders respecting land in another jurisdiction. In some jurisdictions, the family property legislation authorizes judges to adjust any distribution of family property to take account of the value of property in other jurisdictions, or governed by federal or First Nations laws.

Rights and obligations of intimate partners created or confirmed by provincial and territorial legislation apply only to those intimate partnerships that are recognized in the legislation. Most family property legislation speaks of spouses, a term that would include only legally married same-sex and opposite sex partners, unless the legislation defined the term to include other intimate partnerships. The Supreme Court ruled in *Nova Scotia (Attorney General) v. Walsh*, [2002] S.C.J. No. 84, [2002] 4 S.C.R. 325 (S.C.C.) that excluding unmarried intimate partners from family property legislation was discrimination that was justified, given the purpose of family property legislation. Thus, unmarried cohabitees may be able to assert claims for support under provincial or territorial legislation, but, unless their relationships are specifically included in family property legislation, unmarried cohabitees can claim rights in family property to which they do not hold title only if they create those rights themselves in a domestic contract, or if they can establish the necessary factual basis for a beneficial interest by way of constructive trust, as discussed in Chapter Nine. Married partners, too, may make ownership claims based on resulting or constructive trust in order to share in a post-separation increase in the value of property to which their partner holds title, unless such claims are barred, as in Prince Edward Island, by family property legislation.

## HISTORICAL DEVELOPMENT

At common law, husband and wife were regarded as one person, and that person was the husband. A married woman, regarded in law as being under the protection of her husband, could not make binding contracts or bring lawsuits without her husband's concurrence. A married man gained the right to manage and take the profits of his wife's real property, and became outright owner, with full powers of use and disposition, of all of her personal property except her paraphernalia. Even a married woman's wages belonged to her husband. In Blackstone's cogent summary: "By marriage, the husband and wife are one person in law: that is, the very being or legal existence of the woman is suspended during the marriage, or at least is incorporated and consolidated into that of the husband: under whose wing, protection, and *cover*, she performs everything." (1 Bl. Comm. 441) Marriage for the wife thus resulted in a change in her civil status from *feme sole* to *feme covert*.

Although the husband acquired substantial rights over his wife's real property, a wife acquired no similar rights over her husband's property. However, if she survived him, she became entitled to dower, that is, a life estate in one-third of all the freehold estates of inheritance of which her husband had been solely seised at any time during the marriage. Because of the wife's inchoate dower right, the husband could not alienate property he acquired during the marriage without having his wife join in the conveyance to bar her dower.

The common law regime of family property meant that fathers could not convey property to their daughters without risk that it might be dissipated by fortune-seeking husbands, so conveyancers created the wife's separate property in equity. By the end of the 16th century, and quite commonly in the 18th and 19th centuries, married women from propertied families were able to retain some property for themselves through conveyances to uses. To keep the wife's property out of reach of her husband and his creditors, the donor transferred legal title to the property to a trustee for the wife's "separate use". The wife, as *cestui que trust*, had the power to dispose of her separate property by deed or will; she could enter into contracts with respect to it and she could order that it be conveyed to a third party or to herself. Creating valid settlements, whereby a married woman could enjoy separate property in equity, required both property to settle and resort to a solicitor to draft the necessary instruments, and thus was beyond the means of many families.

In the last half of the 19th century, after a long campaign for legislation recognizing married women's right to their own property, various common law jurisdictions enacted Married Women's Property Acts providing a statutory regime of separate property without the necessity of creating trusts. Like the statutory reforms of family property law in the Canadian common law jurisdictions a century later, the Married Women's Property Acts had contradictory consequences. Under a separate property regime, each spouse was entitled to what that spouse owned. Property claims were based on title, not on rights and obligations arising from the marital relationship. Women without means could be left without property under the separate property regime, for unless they held title to property acquired during the marriage, they had no claim to share in it.

Under the *Civil Code of Lower Canada*, which came into force in 1866, married women in Québec suffered the same legal disabilities as the *feme covert* under the common law doctrine of marital unity, but married women in Québec had greater rights to share in family property. As head of the household, the husband had the right to manage the family property, but personal property brought into the marriage, as well as most of the property acquired during the marriage, belonged to both spouses. This legal regime was called "community of property", and governed property relations between spouses unless the spouses by a contract substituted another regime. In 1931, the Québec legislature modified the community of property regime to create a new category of property reserved for management by the wife. Like the Married Women's Property Acts, the change gave married women rights to manage the proceeds of their personal work and any property purchased with their own savings.

## MODERN FAMILY PROPERTY REGIMES

In 1970, the Québec legislature replaced community of property with a new legal regime called "partnership of acquests", designed to recognize marriage as a joint economic venture, and to provide for sharing of assets acquired by the spouses, with equal division of property on marriage breakdown or death. The common law jurisdictions were also considering revisions to the separate property regime. Despite differences in conceptualization, terminology and procedure between the civil law and the common law, the two legal systems adopted similar responses to similar problems. For the most part, the regimes leave married couples free to manage their property separately while the spouses are living together amicably. But on marriage breakdown, each spouse is entitled to an equal share of the property defined as family property, regardless of which spouse is the owner.

Family property legislation provides no uniform definition of what property is included in the property to be divided. Some jurisdictions exclude business assets but include all property used by the family for family purposes, whenever acquired. Others exclude property brought to the marriage, but include property acquired during the marriage, whatever its use. Some jurisdictions mandate division by way of an equalization payment, with the spouse who owns more property making a cash payment to the other to equalize their shares. Other jurisdictions provide for dividing the property *in specie*, by dividing actual assets rather than their cash equivalent, so that, for example, one spouse keeps the cottage and boat and the other the family home. All jurisdictions give judges some discretion to order unequal division in circumstances in which equal division would be unfair, considering such things as each spouse's contribution to the marriage or to the acquisition or maintenance of the family property. Of course, if partners can agree, they can make their own choices about an appropriate property division in a separation agreement.

## RIGHTS IN THE FAMILY HOME

### Ownership Rights

Only in Newfoundland and Labrador, and New Brunswick do spouses acquire immediate ownership rights in the family home as an incident of the marriage. In New Brunswick, regardless of how title is held, each spouse is entitled to half of the proceeds from the sale of a family home, subject to the court's authority to order an unequal division in some circumstances. In Newfoundland and Labrador, on marriage, each spouse acquires a half interest in the family home owned by either or both spouses, regardless of which spouse holds title. In British Columbia, ownership follows title while the spouses are living together, but on marriage breakdown, each spouse receives an undivided one-half interest in all family assets, including the family home.

### Limits on the Owner's Right to Dispose of any Interest in the Family Home

The dower right protected the wife from having her home sold without her knowledge, and protected the widow from losing her home on her husband's death. Homestead legislation in western Canada and family property legislation elsewhere replaced the dower right with prohibitions on a spouse's right to convey any interest in the family home, including a security interest by way of a mortgage, without the consent of the other spouse.

## Orders for Exclusive Possession

All of the Canadian jurisdictions authorize judges to make orders giving a spouse the exclusive possession of the family home, even if such an order deprives a title-holding spouse of the right to possession that ordinarily comes with ownership. Such orders are generally linked to the best interests of the children, pending decisions on a final distribution of family property on marriage breakdown. An order granting one spouse exclusive possession of a family home generally creates a personal right against the other spouse, not a property right. Nonetheless, an order for exclusive possession can be registered against the title to the land in Alberta, Ontario and Prince Edward Island.

# Appendix A
# Analyzing the Validity of Conveyances

First determine the kind of interest. Then consider whether the Rule in *Shelley's Case* applies.
Then do the step-by-step analysis.

## Equitable Executory Interest

**Common law remainder rules do not apply to:**

- Devises (treated as equitable interests in most jurisdictions)
- Uses not executed by the *Statute of Uses* where the
  - trustee a leaseholder
  - trustee a corporation
  - trustee has active duties
  - form of conveyance is "Unto and to the use of"

The only question is whether interest violates Rule against Perpetuities.

## Legal Remainder

Is interest void *ab initio* because it violates the common law remainder rules? If yes, remainder void, end of inquiry. If no, then:

Is interest vested or contingent? If vested, end of inquiry — *i.e.*, interest valid. If contingent,

## Legal Executory Interest

**Does Rule in *Purefoy v. Rogers* require that interest be treated as legal remainder?**

- If would be valid vested interest under common law remainder rules — valid. End of inquiry.
- If is contingent interest that could be valid under common law remainder rules (wait-and-see situation) — treat as legal remainder.
- If would be void *ab initio* under common law remainder rules, not subject to common law remainder rules — valid unless violates Rule Against Perpetuities.

Will interest vest during or at end of prior particular estate? If it cannot, interest void. If it can, interest valid unless it violates Rule Against Perpetuities; *i.e.*, if prior particular estate is given to life in being, interest cannot violate Rule Against Perpetuites. If not,

Is there any possibility, however remote, that interest might vest more than 21 years after the death of lives in being? If yes, interest is void *ab initio*. No wait-and-see.

# Review Problems

Some things you learn best by doing, and drafting grants is among them. These exercises will help you review and test your knowledge of the various rules that you have learned. The goal is to understand how the rules operate so that you can use them to achieve the results that your clients want, and avoid unexpected, unwanted results. After working through the problems and checking the answers, go a step further, and figure out how to redraft any defective grant to achieve, as nearly as possible, the grantor's intentions.

These problems are divided into two parts, with answers and explanation following each part. The first part presents the problems in a structured format that helps you focus on which rules apply, and why. The second part presents problems in random order. The instructions for both parts are given below, following the review of the principles to apply.

Remember that the legal remainder rule requiring timely vesting is a wait-and-see rule (the grant will vest in interest if someone meets the condition for vesting during the prior particular estate), but the rule against perpetuities is not a wait-and-see rule. The latter rule requires that we determine, on the effective date of the grant, based on the possibilities that exist at that time, whether vesting of a contingent interest can occur, if at all, only within 21 years of the death of the relevant lives in being. Note that we do not have to know if the interest will vest within the permitted period — only that the condition for vesting cannot be met outside of that period. If we cannot say with certainty that the condition for vesting must be met, if at all, only within the period permitted by the rule against perpetuities, then the part of the grant that violates the rule is void, even if, had we waited, the interest would have vested in the permitted time period.

Different forms of grants create different kinds of estates or interests in land. You have to identify the kind of interest or estate that you have in order to know what rules apply. The possibilities are:

**1. Legal Remainders (also called common law remainders)**

*Example*: To A for life, remainder to B in fee simple.

In a common law or legal grant without any uses or trusts, the grantee receives both the legal and the equitable title. The common law remainder rules and the rule against perpetuities apply.

### 2. Legal Executory Interests

*Example*: To T in fee simple in trust for A for life, and then in trust for B in fee simple.

To T in fee simple to the use of A for life, and then to the use of B in fee simple.

A conveyance to the uses that is executed by the *Statute of Uses, 1535* (U.K.), 27 Hen. 8, c. 10, converts legal remainders to legal executory interests. What would have been a remainder in a common law grant becomes a legal executory interest. The legal remainder rules apply, according to the rule in *Purefoy v. Rogers* (1671), 85 E.R. 1181, only if the legal executory interest could vest in compliance with the legal remainder rules. (If it can, it must.) The remainder rules do not apply to those legal executory interests that would have been void *ab initio* if they had been legal remainders. (If it cannot, it need not.) The rule against perpetuities applies in any case.

### 3. Equitable Interests

*Example*: Unto and to the use of T in fee simple in trust for/to the use of/ A for life, and then in trust for/to the use of/ B in fee simple.

To T Ltd. in fee simple in trust for/to the use of/ A for life, and then in trust for/to the use of/ B in fee simple.

To T in fee simple to collect the rents and profits for the use of/in trust for/ A for life, and then for the use of/in trust for/ B in fee simple.

To T for 999 years in trust for/to the use of/ A for life, and then in trust for/to the use of/ B in fee simple.

The trustee retains the legal estate and the beneficiary of the trust receives the equitable interest in a conveyance to the uses that is not executed by the *Statute of Uses*. Most commonly, drafters ensure that legal and equitable interests will remain separate by using the "unto and to the use" formula. Execution of uses by the *Statute of Uses* is avoided as well if the trustee is a corporation (To A Ltd. to the use of A); has active duties (*e.g.*, to A in fee simple to mow the grass, clear away the snow, clean the eaves, collect the rents and pay the profits to B); or if the trustee holds a leasehold rather than a freehold estate (to A for 999 years).

The legal remainder rules do not apply to equitable executory interests. The rule against perpetuities does.

## INSTRUCTIONS

In the following *inter vivos* grants, identify the estate or interest in land received by each of the named grantees and any estate or interest in land retained by the grantor. (The answer may be nothing.) Assume that all of these grants are made after passage of legislation recognizing the words "in fee simple" as creating a fee simple estate. Assume as well that if the grant lacks appropriate words of limitation, the default is creation of a life estate. Treat references to reaching a specified age as conditions for vesting in interest. Apply the unmodified common law rule against perpetuities. Unless you are told otherwise, assume that a person identified by name is alive at the effective date of the grant, *i.e.*, the date that the instrument containing the grant is signed, sealed and delivered. Assume that all of the conditions are certain enough to be enforceable, and that none offend against public policy or create an undue restraint on alienation.

## Part I: Recognizing that Different Legal Consequences Flow From Different Facts

As you work through the grants in Part I, note that:

1. The conveyances are arranged in five sets, based on the factual circumstances of the condition precedent for vesting, the factual circumstances of the grantees of the estate with a condition precedent for vesting, or the factual circumstances of the holders of the estate that is the prior particular estate for the estate with a condition precedent for vesting. The correct analysis is fact-dependent: you have to read and understand the facts before you can apply the law.

2. Each of the sets contains four different kinds of conveyances, in the same order in each set. All are subject to the rule against perpetuities, *i.e.*, you must ask with each whether the rule against perpetuities will void any contingent interests.

The first conveyance in each set is an ordinary common law conveyance, with no separation of the legal and equitable estates (To A for life . . .).

The second conveyance in each set is a conveyance to uses that is not executed by the *Statute of Uses*. Beginning a grant with the "unto and to the use" formula is one way to avoid the operation of the *Statute of Uses* and maintain the separation of legal and equitable interests. Equitable executory interests are not subject to the legal remainder rules.

The third conveyance in each set is a conveyance to the uses that is executed by the *Statute of Uses*. The Statute takes the legal title from the person named as trustee and re-unites it with the equitable title that the grant gives to the beneficiaries of the trust. (To T in fee simple to the use of/in trust for/ A for life . . .). The third conveyance in each set is structured so that IF the legal executory interests were legal remainders, they would NOT be void *ab initio* under the legal remainder rules, and therefore, according to the rule in *Purefoy v. Rogers*, they must be treated as legal remainders. Thus, all of the legal executory interests in the third conveyance in each set MUST comply with the legal remainder rules (if it can, it must).

The fourth conveyance in each set is also a conveyance to the uses that is executed by the *Statute of Uses*. These grants are structured so that IF the legal executory interests were legal remainders, they would be void *ab initio* under the legal remainder rules, and therefore, according to the rule in *Purefoy v Rogers*, they need NOT comply with the legal remainder rules (if it cannot, it need not).

**Set A: Note that the condition for vesting in interest is one that can be met, if at all, only within the lifetime of a life in being — Jane.**

1. To Alice for life, then to Jane in fee simple when Jane becomes a member of the Barristers' Society.

2. Unto and to the use of Tom in fee simple in trust for Alice for life, then in trust for Jane in fee simple when Jane becomes a member of the Barristers' Society.

3. To Tom in fee simple in trust for Alice for life, then in trust for Jane in fee simple when Jane becomes a member of the Barristers' Society.

4. To Tom in fee simple in trust for Alice for life, then in trust for Jane in fee simple at least one month after Alice's death, when Jane becomes a member of the Barristers' Society.

**Set B: Note that the condition for vesting in interest is one that can be met, if at all, only within the lifetime of a life in being — the current leader of the Green Party.**

5. To Alice for life, then to Jane in fee simple when the current leader of the Green Party becomes Prime Minister of Canada.

6. Unto and to the use of Tom in fee simple in trust for Alice for life, then in trust for Jane in fee simple when the current leader of the Green Party becomes Prime Minister of Canada.

7. To Tom in fee simple in trust for Alice for life, then in trust for Jane in fee simple when the current leader of the Green Party becomes Prime Minister of Canada.

8. To Tom in fee simple in trust for Alice for life, then in trust for Jane in fee simple at least one month after Alice's death, when the current leader of the Green Party becomes Prime Minister of Canada.

**Set C: Note that the condition for vesting is one that might be met beyond the lifetime of either Alice or Jane, the only relevant lives in being. Note, too, that if Jane dies before the interest vests, the possibility of its vesting dies with her.**

9. To Alice for life, then to Jane in fee simple when the Green Party forms the government in Ottawa.

10. Unto and to the use of Tom in fee simple in trust for Alice for life, then in trust for Jane in fee simple when the Green Party forms the government in Ottawa.

11. To Tom in fee simple in trust for Alice for life, then in trust for Jane in fee simple when the Green Party forms the government in Ottawa.

12. To Tom in fee simple in trust for Alice for life, then in trust for Jane in fee simple at least one month after Alice's death, when the Green Party forms the government in Ottawa.

**Set D: Note that, as Alice is still alive, she could have more children, so the grantee of the remainder or executory interest is not necessarily a life in being at the effective date of the grant.**

13. To Alice for life, then in fee simple to the first of Alice's children to become a member of the Barristers' Society.

14. Unto and to the use of Tom in fee simple in trust for Alice for life, then in trust in fee simple for the first of Alice's children to become a member of the Barristers' Society.

15. To Tom in fee simple in trust for Alice for life, then in trust in fee simple for the first of Alice's children to become a member of the Barristers' Society.

16. To Tom in fee simple in trust for Alice for life, then in trust in fee simple at least one month after Alice's death for the first of Alice's children to become a member of the Barristers' Society.

**Set E: Note that, as Alice is still alive, and could have more children, the holders of the second prior particular estate (life estate to Alice's children) are not necessarily lives in being at the effective date of the grant. Thus, even though the condition of reaching the age of 21 is one that all of Alice's grandchildren must meet within 21 years of the death of that grandchild's parent, that is not necessarily within 21 years of the death of a life in being.**

17. To Alice for life, then to Alice's children for life, then in fee simple to Alice's first grandchild to reach the age of 21.

18. Unto and to the use of Tom in fee simple in trust for Alice for life, then in trust for Alice's children for life, then in trust for Alice's first grandchild to reach the age of 21.

19. To Tom in fee simple in trust for Alice for life, then in trust for Alice's children for life, then in trust for Alice's first grandchild to reach the age of 21.

20. To Tom in fee simple in trust for Alice for life, then in trust for Alice's children for life, then at least one month after the death of Alice's last surviving child, in trust for Alice's first grandchild to reach the age of 21.

## Part I: Answers and Explanations

When you have reviewed these answers, test your knowledge by analysing the following variants on these grants, paying attention to how the changed possibilities arising from the different facts will change the impact of the rule against perpetuities.

1. Replace "Jane" in all of the grants with "Alice's daughters", assuming that Alice is alive at the effective date of the grant.

2. Replace "Jane" in all of the grants with "Jane's daughters", assuming that Jane is dead at the effective date of the grant.

3. After the life estate to Alice, add a life estate to Alice's first-born daughter. Analyze this grant based on two different assumptions:

(a) on the assumption that Alice has a daughter at the effective date of the grant; and

(b) on the assumption that Alice does not have any daughters at the effective date of the grant.

**Set A**

**1. To Alice for life, then to Jane in fee simple when Jane becomes a member of the Barristers' Society.**

Alice: legal and equitable life estate, vesting in interest and possession at effective date of grant; Alice has seisin during her life estate.

Jane: legal and equitable remainder in fee simple, contingent on becoming a member of the Barristers' Society <u>before Alice dies</u>; will vest in interest when meets condition and in possession on Alice's death.

Grantor or grantor's estate: legal and equitable fee simple in reversion if Jane does not meet the condition; will vest in interest when clear that Jane will not meet condition (either death of Jane during Alice's lifetime before meeting condition, or death of Alice during Jane's lifetime before Jane meets condition) and will vest in possession on Alice's death.

**2. Unto and to the use of Tom in fee simple in trust for Alice for life, then in trust for Jane in fee simple when Jane becomes a member of the Barristers' Society.**

Tom: legal fee simple to hold on trust for beneficiaries of grant; Tom has seisin throughout.

Alice: equitable life estate, vesting in interest and possession at effective date of grant.

Jane: equitable executory interest contingent on becoming a member of the Barristers' Society; if Jane meets condition while Alice is still alive, interest will vest in interest then and in possession on Alice's death; if Jane meets the condition after Alice dies, interest will vest in interest and possession then.

Grantor or grantor's estate: equitable executory interest in fee simple if Jane has not met condition at Alice's death, subject to divestment when Jane meets the condition; if Jane dies without meeting condition, grantor's equitable fee simple no longer subject to divestment.

**3. To Tom in fee simple in trust for Alice for life, then in trust for Jane in fee simple when Jane becomes a member of the Barristers' Society.**

Tom: legal fee simple for a scintilla of time, until *Statute of Uses* executes the uses.

Alice: legal and equitable life estate, vesting in interest and possession at the effective date of the grant; Alice has seisin during her life estate.

Jane: legal executory interest in fee simple contingent on becoming a member of the Barristers' Society before Alice dies: if Jane meets condition while Alice is still alive, interest will vest in interest then and in possession on Alice's death (*Purefoy v. Rogers* requires that grant comply with common law remainder rules).

Grantor or grantor's estate: legal executory interest in fee simple if Jane does not meet the condition within Alice's lifetime; will vest in interest when clear that Jane will not meet condition (death of Jane during Alice's lifetime before meeting condition or death of Alice during Jane's lifetime before Jane meets condition) and will vest in possession on Alice's death.

**4. To Tom in fee simple in trust for Alice for life, then in trust for Jane in fee simple at least one month after Alice's death, when Jane becomes a member of the Barristers' Society.**

Tom: legal fee simple for a scintilla of time, until *Statute of Uses* executes the uses.

Alice: legal and equitable life estate, vesting in interest and possession at the effective date of the grant; Alice has seisin during her life estate.

Jane: legal executory interest in fee simple contingent on becoming a member of the Barristers' Society; if Jane meets condition while Alice is still alive, interest will vest in interest then and in possession on Alice's death (*Purefoy v. Rogers* does not require that grant comply with common law remainder rules, because as a common law remainder, it would be void *ab initio* because of the built-in gap in seisin); if Jane meets the condition after Alice dies, interest will vest in interest and possession then.

Grantor or grantor's estate: legal executory interest in fee simple if Jane has not met condition at Alice's death, subject to divestment when Jane meets the condition; if Jane dies without meeting condition, grantor's legal and equitable fee simple no longer subject to divestment.

**Set B**

**5. To Alice for life, then to Jane in fee simple when the current leader of the Green Party becomes Prime Minister of Canada.**

Alice: legal and equitable life estate, vesting in interest and possession at effective date of grant.

Jane: legal and equitable fee simple if the current leader of the Green Parrty becomes Prime Minister of Canada <u>during Alice's lifetime</u>.

Grantor or grantor's estate: legal and equitable fee simple in reversion if the current leader of the Green Party has not become Prime Minister of Canada during Alice's and Jane's lifetime, vesting in interest when the current leader of the Green Party dies without becoming Prime Minister, or on death of Alice, whichever is later, or on death of Jane prior to either event.

**6. Unto and to the use of Tom in fee simple in trust for Alice for life, then in trust for Jane in fee simple when the current leader of the Green Party becomes Prime Minister of Canada.**

Tom: legal fee simple.

Alice: equitable life estate, vesting in interest and in possession at effective date of grant.

Jane: equitable fee simple if the current leader of the Green Party becomes Prime Minister during Jane's lifetime, vesting in interest when that happens and in possession then, too, if Alice is dead and if she is not, then on her death.

Grantor or grantor's estate: equitable executory interest in fee simple vesting in interest and possession at end of Alice's life estate if the current leader of the Green Party has not become Prime Minister by then; subject to divestment if the current leader of the Green Party becomes Prime Minister during Jane's lifetime.

**7. To Tom in fee simple in trust for Alice for life, then in trust for Jane in fee simple when the current leader of the Green Party becomes Prime Minister of Canada.**

Tom: legal fee simple for a scintilla of time, until *Statute of Uses* executes the uses.

Alice: legal and equitable life estate, vesting in interest and possession at effective date of grant.

Jane: legal executory interest in fee simple vesting in interest if the current leader of the Green Party becomes Prime Minister during Alice's lifetime, and vesting in possession when Alice dies.

Grantor or Grantor's estate: legal executory interest in fee simple if the current leader of the Green Party has not become Prime Minister of Canada during Alice's and Jane's lifetime, vesting in interest when the current leader of the Green Party dies without becoming Prime Minister, or on death of Alice, whichever is later; or on death of Jane prior to either event.

**8. To Tom in fee simple in trust for Alice for life, then in trust for Jane in fee simple at least one month after Alice's death, when the current leader of the Green Party becomes Prime Minister of Canada.**

Tom: legal fee simple for a scintilla of time, until *Statute of Uses* executes the uses.

Alice: legal and equitable life estate, vested in interest and possession at effective date of grant.

Jane: legal executory interest in fee simple vesting in interest if the current leader of the Green Party becomes Prime Minister during Jane's lifetime, vesting in interest when that happens and in possession then, too, if Alice is dead, and if she is not, then on her death.

Grantor or Grantor's estate: legal executory interest in fee simple vesting in interest and possession at end of Alice's life estate if the current leader of the Green Party has not become Prime Minister of Canada by then;

subject to divestment if the current leader of the Green Party becomes Prime Minster during Jane's lifetime.

**Set C**

**9. To Alice for life, then to Jane in fee simple when the Green Party forms the government in Ottawa.**

Alice: legal and equitable life estate, vesting in interest and possession at effective date of grant.

Jane: legal and equitable fee simple in remainder if Green Party forms the government in Ottawa during Alice's lifetime.

Grantor or Grantor's estate: legal and equitable fee simple in reversion vesting in interest and possession on Alice's death if Green Party has not formed the government in Ottawa (will vest in interest on Jane's death if Jane predeceases Alice before Green Party forms government).

**10. Unto and to the use of Tom in fee simple in trust for Alice for life, then in trust for Jane in fee simple when the Green Party forms the government in Ottawa.**

Tom: legal fee simple.

Alice: equitable life estate, vesting in interest and possession at effective date of grant.

Jane: equitable executory interest in fee simple whenever Green Party forms the government in Ottawa.

Grantor or Grantor's estate: equitable executory interest in fee simple vesting in interest and possession on Alice's death if Green Party has not formed the government in Ottawa, subject to divestment if Green Party forms the government in Ottawa during Jane's lifetime.

**11. To Tom in fee simple in trust for Alice for life, then in trust for Jane in fee simple when the Green Party forms the government in Ottawa.**

Tom: legal fee simple for a scintilla of time, until *Statute of Uses* executes uses.

Alice: legal and equitable life estate, vested in interest and possession at effective date of grant.

Jane: legal executory interest in fee simple if Green Party has formed the government in Ottawa during Alice's lifetime.

Grantor or Grantor's estate: legal executory interest in fee simple vesting in interest and possession on Alice's death if Green Party has not formed the government in Ottawa (will vest in interest on Jane's death if she predeceases Alice before Green Party forms government).

**12. To Tom in fee simple in trust for Alice for life, then in trust for Jane in fee simple at least one month after Alice's death, when the Green Party forms the government in Ottawa.**

Tom: legal fee simple for a scintilla of time, until *Statute of Uses* executes uses.

Alice: legal and equitable life estate, vested in interest and possession at effective date of grant.

Jane: legal executory interest in fee simple if Green Party forms the government in Ottawa.

Grantor or Grantor's estate: legal executory interest in fee simple on Alice's death if Green Party has not formed the government in Ottawa during Alice's lifetime, subject to divestment if Green Party forms the government in Ottawa during Jane's lifetime.

**Set D**

**13. To Alice for life, then in fee simple to the first of Alice's children to become a member of the Barristers' Society.**

Alice: legal and equitable life estate.

First of Alice's children to become a member of the Barristers' Society within Alice's lifetime: legal and equitable fee simple in remainder.

Grantor or Grantor's estate: legal and equitable fee simple in reversion if none of Alice's children becomes a member of the Barristers' Society within Alice's lifetime.

**14. Unto and to the use of Tom in fee simple in trust for Alice for life, then in trust in fee simple for the first of Alice's children to become a member of the Barristers' Society.**

Tom: legal fee simple.

Alice: equitable life estate.

First of Alice's children to become a member of the Barristers' Society: nothing — perpetuities problem.

Grantor or Grantor's estate: equitable fee simple vested in interest at effective date of grant and vested in possession on Alice's death.

**15. To Tom in fee simple in trust for Alice for life, then in trust in fee simple for the first of Alice's children to become a member of the Barristers' Society.**

Tom: legal fee simple for a scintilla of time.

Alice: legal and equitable life estate.

First of Alice's children to become a member of the Barristers' Society within Alice's lifetime: legal executory interest in fee simple.

Grantor or Grantor's estate: legal executory interest in fee simple on Alice's death if none of Alice's children has become a member of the Barristers' Society within Alice's lifetime.

**16. To Tom in fee simple in trust for Alice for life, then in trust in fee simple at least one month after Alice's death for the first of Alice's children to become a member of the Barristers' Society.**

Tom: legal fee simple for a scintilla of time.

Alice: legal and equitable life estate.

First of Alice's children to become a member of the Barristers' Society: nothing — perpetuities problem.

Grantor or Grantor's estate: legal and equitable interest in fee simple vested in interest at effective date of grant and vested in possession on Alice's death.

**Set E**

**17. To Alice for life, then to Alice's children for life, then in fee simple to Alice's first grandchild to reach the age of 21.**

Alice: legal and equitable life estate.

Alice's children: legal and equitable life estate vesting in interest at effective date of grant for children alive then and when they are born for children born after effective date of grant, and vesting in possession on Alice's death.

Alice's first grandchild to reach 21: nothing — perpetuities problem.

Grantor or Grantor's estate: legal and equitable fee simple in reversion vesting in interest on date of grant and in possession on death of longest-living of Alice's children.

**18. Unto and to the use of Tom in fee simple in trust for Alice for life, then in trust for Alice's children for life, then in trust for Alice's first grandchild to reach the age of 21.**

Tom: legal fee simple.

Alice: equitable life estate.

Alice's children: equitable life estate vesting in interest at effective date of grant for children alive then and when they are born for children born after effective date of grant, and vesting in possession on Alice's death.

Alice's first grandchild to reach 21: nothing — perpetuities problem.

Grantor or Grantor's estate: equitable executory interest in fee simple vesting in interest on date of grant and in possession on death of longest-living of Alice's children.

**19. To Tom in fee simple in trust for Alice for life, then in trust for Alice's children for life, then in trust for Alice's first grandchild to reach the age of 21.**

Tom: legal fee simple for a scintilla of time.

Alice: legal and equitable life estate.

Alice's children: legal and equitable life estate vesting in interest at effective date of grant for children alive then and when they are born for children born after effective date of grant, and vesting in possession on Alice's death.

Alice's first grandchild to reach 21: nothing — perpetuities problem.

Grantor or Grantor's estate: legal executory interest in fee simple vesting in interest on the effective date of grant and in possession on death of longest-living of Alice's children.

**20. To Tom in fee simple in trust for Alice for life, then in trust for Alice's children for life, then at least one month after the death of Alice's last surviving child, in trust for Alice's first grandchild to reach the age of 21.**

Tom: legal fee simple for a scintilla of time.

Alice: legal and equitable life estate.

Alice's children: legal and equitable life estate vesting in interest at effective date of grant for children alive then and when they are born for children born after effective date of grant, and vesting in possession on Alice's death.

Alice's first grandchild to reach 21: nothing — perpetuities problem.

Grantor or Grantor's estate: legal executory interest in fee simple vesting in interest on effective date of grant and in possession on death of longest-living of Alice's children.

## Part II: Random Problems

1. P grants to A for 10 years, to the use of B for 10 years.
2. P grants to A and her heirs to the use of B for life, and then to the use of the Clearcut Paper Corporation.
3. P grants to A, then to B, remainder in fee simple to A's heirs.
4. P grants to B and his heirs to the use of C in fee simple to the use of D and her heirs.
5. P grants to XYZ Corporation to the use of B for life.
6. P grants unto and to the use of A and his heirs to the use of B for life and then to the use of C and her heirs.
7. P grants to A for life, remainder unto and to the use of B and his heirs for the use of A's heirs and their heirs.
8. P grants to A for the life of A's spouse.
9. P grants to B for life, and after his death to B's heirs.
10. P grants unto and to the use of T in fee simple to the use of B for life, then to the use of B's children.
11. P grants to B for life, then to C for life, then to C's eldest child for the life of C.
12. P grants unto and to the use of B and his heirs to the use of C for life.
13. P grants to B and her heirs in trust to collect the rents and profits and to pay them to C during her life, and on the death of C, to pay the rents and profits to the heirs of C in fee simple.
14. P grants to A and her heirs, then to B and her heirs.
15. P grants unto and to the use of A and her heirs to the use of B and her heirs.
16. P grants to A for 21 years, remainder to B and her heirs.
17. P grants to A for 999 years to the use of B for life, then to the use of C in fee simple.
18. P grants to A and his heirs to collect the rents and profits and to pay them to B during her lifetime, and, on her death, to convey the title to C and her heirs.
19. P grants to A for life, and then to A's surviving children forever.

20. P grants to A for life, and then in fee simple to the first of P's children to get a full-time, permanent job.

21. P grants to A in fee simple, to the use of B for life, remainder to the use of B's eldest daughter in fee simple when she is 21.

22. P grants unto and to the use of A in fee simple, in trust for B for life when B is 21.

23. P grants to A for life, and then to B and her heirs so long as she farms the land, then in fee simple to C.

24. P grants to A for life and then to B and her heirs providing she graduates from veterinary college, and, if she does not, then to C in fee simple.

25. P grants to A for life, and then to B in fee simple providing that she does not marry until after A's death.

26. P grants to A for life and then in fee simple to A's children who have graduated from the Faculty of Law.

27. P grants to the Trust T Corporation to the use of A for life, then to the use of A's children in fee simple, when they graduate from the Faculty of Law, providing they do so within 21 years of the death of the current Dean.

28. P grants unto and to the use of T in fee simple, in trust for A for life, then in trust for A's children in fee simple, no matter when they are born.

29. P grants to T in fee simple to the use of L for life, provided that L does not use the property for the purposes of manufacturing or selling alcohol; and if L does use the property for those purposes, then to the use of M for life, and then, on the termination of the life estates, to the use of N and her heirs.

30. P grants to the XYZ Corporation in fee simple, in trust for A for life, then in trust for the Faculty of Law in fee simple when half of the full-time teaching faculty are women.

31. P grants to T in fee simple, in trust for A for life, then in trust for the Faculty of Law in fee simple when half of the full-time teaching faculty are women.

32. P grants to A for life, then to the Faculty of Law in fee simple when half of the full-time teaching faculty are women, providing this condition is met within 21 years of the death of the current Dean.

33. P grants to X for life, the remainder in fee simple to the first child of X to reach the age of 25.

34. P grants unto and to the use of T in fee simple in trust for X for life, then in trust in fee simple to the first child of X to reach the age of 25.

35. P grants to X for life, then to the widow of X for life, then in fee simple to the children of X then living.

36. P grants to X for life, then to M for life, then to M's children then living.

37. P grants to T in fee simple in trust for the first of P's children to graduate from the Faculty of Law.

38. P grants to T in fee simple in trust for A for life, then in trust in fee simple for the eldest daughter of A living at A's death who is a member of the Barristers' Society, but if she is ever disbarred, then in trust in fee simple to the Women's Legal Education and Action Fund.

39. P grants to L for life and then to A and A heirs providing that A is not married to anyone with a degree from a Canadian law school.

40. P grants to L for life and then to A and A heirs providing that A does not marry anyone with a degree from a Canadian law school.

41. P grants to L for life and then to A and heirs, so long as alcohol is not manufactured, sold or consumed on the premises.

42. P grants to L for life and then to A and heirs, providing that the premises are not used for the manufacture, sale or consumption of alcohol.

43. P grants to L for life and then to A in fee simple subject to A's agreement to enroll in the Faculty of Law.

44. P grants to A for 999 years to the use of B in fee simple when B is 21.

45. P grants to A for life, then to A's son, B, for life, then to B's widow for life, then to the use of A's grandchildren and their heirs who reach the age of 21.

46. P grants to A for life, then to A children then surviving for life, then to the use of A's grandchildren and their heirs who reach the age of 21.

47. P grants to A for life, remainder in fee simple to those of A's children surviving at A's death.

48. P grants to A for life, remainder in fee simple to those of A's children who visit A's grave once a week every week for the entire year after A's death.

49. P grants to A for life, remainder in fee simple to those of A's children who reach the age of 31.

50. P grants to T Ltd. in trust for A for life, and one year after A's death to convey the property to those of A's children and their heirs who visited A's grave once a week every week for the entire year after A's death.

51. P grants to T Ltd. in trust for A for life, then in trust for those of A's children and their heirs who reach the age of 31.

52. To T in fee simple on trust for A for life, then on trust for those of A's children and their heirs who reach the age of 31.

## PART II: ANSWERS AND EXPLANATIONS

**1. P grants to A for 10 years, to the use of B for 10 years.**

P: legal and equitable fee simple subject to 10-year lease

A: legal leasehold

B: equitable leasehold

The *Statute of Uses* is avoided because A, the trustee, has a leasehold, and so no one is seised to the use of another.

**2. P grants to A and her heirs to the use of B for life, and then to the use of the Clearcut Paper Corporation.**

P: nothing

A: legal fee simple for a scintilla of time

B: legal and equitable life estate

Clearcut Paper Corp: legal and equitable fee simple, vested in interest at date of grant and in possession on death of B.

The *Statute of Uses* unites legal and equitable title in the hands of the parties who are given equitable estates by grant. No words of limitation are needed to give a fee simple to corporation.

**3. P grants to A, then to B, remainder in fee simple to A's heirs.**

P: nothing

A: legal and equitable life estate, and legal and equitable remainder in fee simple

B: legal and equitable life estate

A's heirs: nothing

*Shelley's Rule* applies because, without any words of limitation in the grant to A, A receives a life estate, followed by an attempt to give a fee simple in remainder to A's whole line of issue. A does not get the immediate fee simple because the intervening life estate to B prevents the operation of the doctrine of merger.

To create a valid fee simple interest in A's children, assuming that is what the grantor intended, revise the grant as follows:

P grants to A for life, then to B for life, remainder in fee simple to A's children.

The word "children" is not interpreted as meaning the whole line of issue, unless the context requires that interpretation, so using that word does not create a problem with the rule in *Shelley's Case* (1581), 1 Co. Rep. 93b. For greater certainty, though, the grantor could add the names of the children. The words "for life" are added for clarity and certainty.

**4. P grants to B and his heirs to the use of C in fee simple to the use of D and her heirs.**

P: nothing

B: legal fee simple for a scintilla of time

C: legal fee simple

D: equitable fee simple

The *Statute of Uses* is exhausted after it executes the first use of the fee simple to C. C has equitable title by the grant and legal title by the operation of the *Statute of Uses*. Legal and equitable title remain separate thereafter, and C holds legal title for the benefit of D.

**5. P grants to XYZ Corporation to the use of B for life.**

P: equitable reversion in fee simple

XYZ Corp.: legal fee simple

B: equitable life estate

A corporation rather than a natural person is seised to the use of another, so the *Statute of Uses* is avoided; legal and equitable title remain separate thereafter. At the end of the express use for the life of B, the trustee will hold the title on a resulting use to the grantor.

**6. P grants unto and to the use of A and his heirs to the use of B for life and then to the use of C and her heirs.**

P: nothing

A: legal fee simple

B: equitable life estate

C: equitable fee simple

Use of the "unto and to the use" formula exhausts the *Statute of Uses* after it executes the use to A; thereafter, legal and equitable title remain separate.

**7. P grants to A for life, remainder unto and to the use of B and his heirs for the use of A's heirs and their heirs.**

P: nothing

A: legal and equitable life estate

B: legal fee simple

A's heirs: equitable fee simple

Although there is a grant of a life estate to the ancestor and a grant of a fee simple to heirs, *Shelley's Rule* does not apply because the grant to A is legal and equitable, while the grant to the heirs is equitable only.

**8. P grants to A for the life of A's spouse.**

P: legal and equitable reversion in fee simple

A: legal and equitable life estate *pur autre vie*

A's spouse: nothing

A's spouse, the *cestui que vie*, is not a grantee; with no grant after the particular estate, the property reverts to the grantor.

**9. P grants to B for life, and after his death to B's heirs.**

P: nothing

B: legal and equitable fee simple

B's heirs: nothing

*Shelley's Rule* applies so B gets a life estate and a fee simple; as there are no intervening estates, B gets an immediate fee simple by the doctrine of merger.

To create a valid fee simple interest in B's children (assuming that is what the grantor intended), revise the grant as follows:

P grants to B for life, and then to B's children.

**10. P grants unto and to the use of T in fee simple to the use of B for life, then to the use of B's children.**

P: equitable reversion in fee simple

T: legal fee simple

B: equitable life estate

B's children: equitable life estate

Use of the "unto and to the use" formula exhausts the *Statute of Uses* after it executes the use to T. *Shelley's Rule* does not apply because "children" is not interpreted as meaning the whole line of issue, unless the context requires that interpretation. Without words of limitation in the grant to B's children, they get a life estate only. On the death of the longest living of B's children, the trustee holds the title for the grantor on a resulting trust.

**11. P grants to B for life, then to C for life, then to C's eldest child for the life of C.**

P: fee simple in reversion at end of C's life estate

B: legal and equitable life estate

C: legal and equitable life estate

C's eldest child: nothing

The grant purports to give C's eldest child a life estate *pur autre vie* but as C is the measuring life, and C must die before the estate to C's eldest child vests in possession, the estate to C's eldest child ends when it begins.

**12. P grants unto and to the use of B and his heirs to the use of C for life.**

P: equitable reversion in fee simple

B: legal fee simple

C: equitable life estate

Use of the "unto and to the use" formula exhausts the *Statute of Uses* after it executes the use to B; thereafter, legal and equitable title remain separate. At the end of C's equitable life estate, B holds legal title on a resulting trust for the grantor.

**13. P grants to B and her heirs in trust to collect the rents and profits and to pay them to C during her life, and on the death of C, to pay the rents and profits to the heirs of C in fee simple.**

P: nothing

B: legal fee simple

C: equitable fee simple

C's heirs: nothing

*Shelley's Rule* applies; the estates to C and to C's heirs are both equitable; the *Statute of Uses* does not execute the use because the trustee has active duties to perform. There is no intervening life estate so C gets the fee simple in possession by the doctrine of merger.

To create a valid fee simple interest in C's children, assuming that is what the grantor intended, revise the grant as follows:

P grants to B and her heirs in trust to collect the rents and profits and to pay them to C during her life, and on the death of C, to pay the rents and profits to C's children and their heirs.

**14. P grants to A and her heirs, then to B and her heirs.**

P: nothing

A: legal and equitable fee simple

B: nothing

Having granted the fee simple to A and her heirs, P has nothing left to grant: no remainder is permitted after a fee simple.

To create a valid interest in B, revise the grant as follows:

P grants to T in fee simple to the use of A and her heirs to the use of B and her heirs (if assume that Grantor wanted A to hold fee simple on trust for B).

**OR** P grants to A for life and then to B and her heirs (if assume that Grantor wanted A to have life estate and B to have fee simple).

**15. P grants unto and to the use of A and her heirs to the use of B and her heirs.**

P: nothing

A: legal fee simple

B: equitable fee simple

Use of the "unto and to the use formula" exhausts the *Statute of Uses* after it executes the use to A; thereafter the legal and equitable title remain separate.

**16. P grants to A for 21 years, remainder to B and her heirs.**

P: nothing

A: legal and equitable leasehold for 21 years

B: legal and equitable fee simple subject to 21-year lease

Seisin goes immediately to B. Despite the wording, B does not get a remainder, but an immediate right to possession, subject to the rights of the leaseholder. The grant of the fee simple is valid even though it is not supported by a prior freehold estate because, with no condition to be met for vesting in interest, it vests in interest immediately.

**17. P grants to A for 999 years to the use of B for life, then to the use of C in fee simple.**

P: legal and equitable reversion in fee simple

A: legal leasehold for 999 years

B: equitable life estate

C: equitable leasehold for balance of 999 years after B's death

The trustee holds a leasehold estate, so no person is seised to the use of another and the *Statute of Uses* is avoided. Legal and equitable title remain separate. C's estate can not be greater than the legal estate which supports it; at end of the 999-year leasehold, legal and equitable title revert to the grantor's estate.

**18. P grants to A and his heirs to collect the rents and profits and to pay them to B during her lifetime, and, on her death, to convey the title to C and her heirs.**

P: nothing

A: legal fee simple

B: equitable life estate

C: legal and equitable fee simple

The trustee has active duties so the *Statute of Uses* is avoided, and legal and equitable title remain separate. A retains legal title to carry out his duties as trustee, including conveying legal title to C.

**19. P grants to A for life, and then to A's surviving children forever.**

P: legal and equitable reversion in fee simple

A: legal and equitable life estate

A's surviving children: legal and equitable life estate

*Shelley's Rule* does not apply because the term "surviving children" does not mean the whole line of issue, but the children do not get fee simple without use of the words "and his heirs" or "in fee simple".

**20. P grants to A for life, and then in fee simple to the first of P's children to get a full-time, permanent job.**

P: legal and equitable reversion in fee simple, if no child qualifies by A's death

A: legal and equitable life estate

First child to get job: contingent remainder in fee simple

In a common law grant, the remainder must vest, if at all, within or at the moment of termination of the prior particular estate. Therefore, there is no perpetuities problem here; even if an after-born child is first to meet the condition, the interest will vest only if the condition is met within the lifetime of A, who is a life in being.

**21. P grants to A in fee simple, to the use of B for life, and then to the use of B's eldest daughter in fee simple when she is 21.**

P: legal and equitable reversion in fee simple if B's eldest daughter is not 21 when B dies

A: legal fee simple for a scintilla of time

B: legal and equitable life estate

B's eldest daughter: legal executory interest in fee simple if she is 21 when B dies

The *Statute of Uses* operates to execute the uses but the legal remainder rules apply to the grant to B's eldest daughter because the grant could take effect as a legal remainder (*Purefoy v. Rogers*). As the grant to B's eldest daughter therefore must vest, if at all, within the prior particular estate, there is no perpetuities problem. Even if the rule in *Purefoy v. Rogers* did not apply, there would not be a perpetuities problem because B's daughter can meet the condition of reaching 21 at the latest within 21 years of B's death.

**22. P grants unto and to the use of A in fee simple, in trust for B for life when B is 21.**

P: equitable fee simple subject to divestment when B reaches 21, equitable reversion in fee simple after B's death

A: legal fee simple

B: equitable executory interest for life when 21

Use of the "unto and to the use" formula exhausts the *Statute of Uses* after it executes the use to A; thereafter legal and equitable title remain separate. The grant to B creates an equitable estate that need not be supported by a prior particular estate. Until B meets the condition, A holds the legal title for the grantor or the grantor's estate on a resulting trust.

**23. P grants to A for life, and then to B and her heirs so long as she farms the land, then in fee simple to C.**

P: possibility of reverter

A: legal and equitable life estate

B: legal and equitable determinable fee simple

C: nothing

In a common law grant, the legal remainder rules apply to invalidate a fee after a fee, even if it is a qualified fee.

To create valid interests, revise as follows:

P grants to A for life, and then to B for life so long as she farms the land, and at the termination of B's estate, to C in fee simple.

This grant creates a fee simple after a determinable life estate, assuming that the requirement that B farm the land is neither void for uncertainty nor void as an undue restraint on alienation. The former is a questionable assumption.

**OR** P grants to T in fee simple to the use of A for life, and then on trust for B in fee simple so long as she farms the land, and if B no longer farms the land, on trust for C in fee simple.

This grant gives C a legal executory interest (equitable interest that is converted to a legal interest by the operation of the *Statute of Uses*), and, because this interest would be void *ab initio* as a legal remainder, according to the rule in *Purefoy v. Rogers*, the legal remainder rules do not apply. Note that because the limitation here is personal to B, *i.e.*, not "so long as the land is used for farming", but "so long as B farms the land", C's interest will vest, if at all, only during B's lifetime, which is within the period permitted by the rule against perpetuities.

**24. P grants to A for life and then to B and her heirs providing she graduates from veterinary college, and if she does not, then to C in fee simple.**

P: nothing

B: contingent remainder in fee simple, which will become vested if B graduates from veterinary college during A's lifetime

C: contingent alternative remainder in fee simple which will vest on A's death if B has not graduated from veterinary college during A's lifetime

The legal remainder rules are not violated because this is not a fee after a fee, but an alternative remainder. B's failing to meet the condition precedent for her gift to vest is the condition precedent for C's gift to vest.

**25. P grants to A for life, and then to B in fee simple on her marriage providing that she does not marry until after A's death.**

P: legal and equitable reversion in fee simple

A: legal and equitable life estate

B: nothing

This is a common law grant so the remainder must comply with the legal remainder rules. The grant to B is void *ab initio* because of the built-in gap in seisin in the condition precedent for B's grant.

To create a valid interest in B, revise as follows:

P grants unto and to the use of T in fee simple to the use of A for life, and then to the use of B in fee simple on her marriage providing that she does not marry until after A's death.

**26. P grants to A for life and then in fee simple to A's children who have graduated from the Faculty of Law.**

P: legal and equitable reversion in fee simple if none of A's children have graduated from the Faculty of Law at A's death

A: legal and equitable life estate

A's children who have graduated from Faculty of Law at A's death: legal and equitable remainder in fee simple

A's children who have not graduated from Faculty of Law at A's death: nothing

As this is a common law grant, the remainder must vest during or at the moment of termination of the prior particular estate; the class closing rules in *Festing v. Allen* (1843), 152 E.R. 1204 (Exch.), will exclude children who qualify late. To extend the time for the children to graduate, convert the interests to equitable interests which are not subject to the legal remainder rules; thus, the class would remain open after the termination of the prior particular estate, and the children who graduate after A dies could share in the gift. However, as these children might be born after the effective date of the grant, and might graduate more than 21 years after the death of A, you need as well to add a time limit for vesting that is within the period permitted by the rule against perpetuities, as follows:

P grants unto and to the use of T in fee simple to the use of A for life, and then to the use of A's children in fee simple who have graduated from the Faculty of Law, providing they do so within 21 years of A's death.

**27. P grants to the Trust T Corporation to the use of A for life, then to the use of A's children in fee simple when they graduate from the Faculty of Law, providing they do so within 21 years of the death of the current Dean.**

P: equitable reversion in fee simple subject to divestment when any of A's children meet condition

Trust T Corporation: legal fee simple

A: equitable life estate

A's first child to graduate from Faculty of Law within the time limit: equitable executory interest in fee simple subject to partial divestment as other children meet condition

A's remaining children to graduate from Faculty of Law within the time limit: equitable executory interest in fee simple shared equally with other children as they meet the condition

The *Statute of Uses* is avoided because a corporation, not a person, is seised to the use of another, so legal and equitable title remain separate. No words of limitation are necessary to give a fee simple to a corporation. The legal remainder rules do not apply to equitable estates, so the class does not close at the termination of the prior particular estate, but there is no perpetuities problem because the grant specifies an appropriate time limit for vesting.

**28. P grants unto and to the use of T in fee simple, in trust for A for life, then in trust for A's children in fee simple, no matter when they are born.**

P: possibility of equitable fee simple in reversion if A has no children

T: legal fee simple

A: equitable life estate

A's children: equitable executory interest in fee simple

Use of the "unto and to the use" formula exhausts the *Statute of Uses* after it executes the use to T, so legal and equitable title remain separate. In an equitable grant, the legal remainder rules do not set a time limit for vesting, but there is no perpetuities problem here because the interest to A's children vests at the latest at A's death plus the gestation period, after which A will not have more children.

**29. P grants to T in fee simple to the use of L for life, provided that L not use the property for the purposes of manufacturing or selling alcohol; and if L does use the property for those purposes, then to**

**the use of M for life, and then, on the termination of the life estates, to the use of N and her heirs.**

P: nothing

T: legal fee simple for a scintilla of time

L: legal and equitable life estate subject to executory limitation

M: legal executory interest for life if L breaches condition

N: legal executory interest in fee simple

If this were a common law grant, the life estate to M would be void because it is contingent on L's estate being cut short by the grantor exercising the right of entry for condition broken. As a legal executory interest, however, it is not subject to the legal remainder rules, but that does not create a perpetuity problem because L can breach the condition only during L's lifetime.

**30. P grants to the XYZ Corporation in fee simple, in trust for A for life, then in trust for the Faculty of Law in fee simple when half of the full-time teaching faculty are women.**

P: equitable reversion in fee simple

XYZ Corporation: legal fee simple

A: equitable life estate

Faculty of Law: nothing

Legal remainder rules do not apply to equitable estates to require that the grant to the Faculty of Law vest during A's life. Because it is possible that the condition precedent for the grant to Faculty of Law might not be met within the perpetuity period (no relevant lives in being here, so period is 21 years from date of grant), the grant is void *ab initio*.

To create a valid interest in the Faculty of Law, revise as follows:
P grants to the XYZ Corporation in fee simple in trust for A for life, then in trust for the Faculty of Law in fee simple when half of the full-time teaching faculty are women, but only if this happens within 21 years of the death of the longest living of the members of the full-time teaching faculty at the date of this grant.

**31. P grants to T in fee simple, in trust for A for life, then in trust for the Faculty of Law in fee simple when half of the full-time teaching faculty are women.**

P: legal and equitable reversion in fee simple if Faculty of Law fails to meet condition

T: legal fee simple for a scintilla of time

A: legal and equitable life estate

UNB Faculty of Law: legal executory interest in fee simple contingent on meeting condition precedent within A's lifetime

Since the grant to the UNB Faculty of Law is a legal executory interest that could vest within A's lifetime, thus taking effect as a legal remainder, under the rule in *Purefoy v. Rogers* it must comply with the legal remainder rules, and vest within A's lifetime, or not at all. As A is a life in being, that means there is no perpetuities problem.

**32. P grants to A for life, then to the Faculty of Law in fee simple when half of the full-time teaching faculty are women, providing this condition is met within 21 years of the death of the current Dean.**

P: legal and equitable reversion in fee simple if Faculty of Law does not meet condition within A's lifetime

A: legal and equitable life estate

Faculty of Law: contingent remainder in fee simple

There is no perpetuity problem here because the legal remainder rules apply; if the condition precedent is not met within A's lifetime, the grant fails; the attempt to protect the grant from the rule against perpetuities by specifying a time limit is unnecessary, and cannot extend the time period for vesting beyond that set by the legal remainder rules.

**33. P grants to X for life, remainder in fee simple to the first child of X to reach the age of 25.**

P: legal and equitable reversion in fee simple if no child of X reaches age of 25 within X's lifetime

X: legal and equitable life estate

First child of X to reach age 25: contingent remainder in fee simple

There is no perpetuity problem here even though X is still alive as the legal remainder rules require X's child's interest to vest, if at all, within X's lifetime.

**34. P grants unto and to the use of T in fee simple in trust for X for life, then in trust in fee simple to the first child of X to reach the age of 25.**

P: equitable reversion in fee simple

T: legal fee simple

X: equitable life estate

First child of X to reach age 25: nothing

Use of "unto and to the use formula" exhausts the *Statute of Uses* after it executes the use to T. The grant to the child is void because of the rule against perpetuities as the legal remainder rules do not apply to require the child's interest to vest during or at the moment of termination of the prior particular estate. The first child of X to reach the age of 25 could do so more than 21 years after X's death, and because X could have more children after the effective date of the grant, the children are not relevant lives in being.

To create a valid interest in X's child, change the required age to 21.

**35. P grants to X for life, then to the widow of X for life, then in fee simple to the children of X then living.**

P: legal and equitable reversion in fee simple

X: legal and equitable life estate

X's widow: legal and equitable life estate on X's death

Children of X then living: nothing

The grant to the children of X is void because it might vest beyond the perpetuity period. We will not know until the death of X's widow which children will be then surviving and that could be more than 21 years after X's death. Becaue it is possible that X might marry someone who was not alive at the effective date of the grant, the widow does not count as a life in being.

To create a valid interest in X's children, revise as follows:

P grants to X for life, then to his widow, Jane, for life, then in fee simple to the children of X then living.

In order to name Jane, she must have been alive at the effective date of the grant, so when the interests of the children vest in interest and possession when Jane dies, that will be within the period permitted by the rule against perpetuities.

**OR**

P grants to X for life, then to X's widow for life, then in fee simple to the children of X.

Without the condition that the children must be living at the death of the widow, the interest of each child will vest in interest when that child is born, and will vest in possession on the death of the widow. As X's children must be born within X's lifetime (plus the gestation period), there is no perpetuity problem.

**36. P grants to X for life, then to M for life, then to M's children then living.**

P: legal and equitable reversion in fee simple

X: legal and equitable life estate

M: legal and equitable life estate

M's children then living: legal and equitable life estate

M's children get a life estate because there are no words of limitation to grant a fee simple. There is no perpetuities problem because M is a life in being and which children meet the condition will be ascertained at M's death.

**37. P grants to T in fee simple in trust for the first of P's children to graduate from the Faculty of Law.**

P: legal and equitable fee simple

T: legal fee simple for a scintilla of time

First child to graduate from Faculty of Law: nothing

The grant to the children would not be valid as a legal remainder because it is not supported by a prior particular estate of freehold, so the rule in *Purefoy v. Rogers* does not apply to set a time limit on vesting. It is possible that the first child to graduate from the Faculty of Law would do so more than 21 years after the death of the grantor; the grantor, not the children, is the relevant life in being because P could have more children after the date of the grant (it is an *inter vivos* grant, not a will). Therefore, the gift to the child is void because of the rule against perpetuities.

To create a valid interest in the first child to meet the condition, revise as follows:

P grants unto and to the use of T in fee simple in trust for the first of P's children now living to graduate from the Faculty of Law. (This grant makes the children lives in being.)

**38. P grants to T in fee simple in trust for A for life, then in trust in fee simple for the eldest daughter of A living at A's death who is a member of the Barristers' Society, but if she is ever disbarred, then in trust in fee simple to the Women's Legal Education and Action Fund (LEAF).**

P: legal and equitable reversion in fee simple if no daughter of A meets condition

T: legal fee simple for a scintilla of time

A: legal and equitable life estate

A's daughter who meets condition at A's death: legal executory interest in fee simple

LEAF: nothing

There is nothing in the grant to block the operation of the *Statute of Uses*, so the uses are executed. The interest to LEAF, as a legal executory interest in fee simple, is not subject to the legal remainder rules prohibiting the grant of a fee after a fee, but it is invalid because of the rule against perpetuities, as the eldest of A's daughters living at A's death might have been born after the effective date of the grant, and might be disbarred more than 21 years after the death of A, the only relevant life in being. The grant to LEAF would be valid **if** A were dead at the effective date of the grant.

To create a valid interest in LEAF, revise as follows:

P grants unto and to the use of T in fee simple in trust for A for life, then in trust in fee simple for the eldest daughter of A now living who is a member of the Barristers' Society, but if she is ever disbarred, then in trust in fee simple to the Women's Legal Education and Action Fund (LEAF).

LEAF, as a corporation, would obtain the fee simple without using words of limitation, but these are added for certainty. Changing the interests from legal executory interests to equitable interests is NOT necessary to save LEAF's interest from the rule against perpetuities, but it is likely that the grantor intended to give equitable interests, as doing so enables the grantor, in a properly drafted grant, to provide for the trustees to manage the estate so as to minimize any conflict among the various grantees.

**39. P grants to L for life and then to A and A heirs providing that A is not married to anyone with a degree from a Canadian law school.**

P: legal and equitable fee simple in reversion if A is married to someone with degree from Canadian law school when L dies

L: legal and equitable life estate

A: legal and equitable fee simple in remainder subject to condition precedent of not being married to anyone with degree from Canadian law school when L dies

This condition could also be a condition subsequent; to argue against that interpretation, focus on grantor's choice of words: grantor used present tense of verb "to be" (is), rather than words that suggest that the condition of not being married must persist into future, *e.g.*, "providing that A is never married to anyone with a degree from a Canadian law school" or "providing that A's spouse does not now and never does hold a degree from a Canadian law school".

**40. P grants to L for life and then to A and A's heirs providing that A does not marry anyone with a degree from a Canadian law school.**

P: legal and equitable reversion in fee simple if A has married someone with degree from Canadian law school by end of L's life, and right of re-entry for condition broken if A violates condition subsequent by marrying someone with a degree from a Canadian law school

L: legal and equitable life estate

A: legal and equitable fee simple in remainder subject to condition precedent of not being married to anyone with degree from Canadian law school, and to condition subsequent of not marrying anyone with a degree from a Canadian law school

**41. P grants to L for life and then to A and heirs, so long as alcohol is not manufactured, sold or consumed on the premises.**

P: possibility of reverter

L: legal and equitable life estate

A: legal and equitable determinable fee simple in remainder

On breach of the conditions concerning use of the land, the possibility of reverter automatically becomes a reality and the property reverts to the grantor or grantor's estate. The possibility of reverter is not subject to the common law rule against perpetuities because the possibility of reverter is not regarded as a contingent interest (but note that in some jurisdictions, legislation may have altered this).

**42. P grants to L for life and then to A and heirs, providing that the premises are not used for the manufacture, sale or consumption of alcohol.**

P: nothing

L: legal and equitable life estate

A: legal and equitable fee simple in remainder

The grantor attempted to grant a fee simple subject to condition subsequent and to retain a right of re-entry, but as the right to exercise this right of re-entry could arise more than 21 years after the death of P or the death of A, the right of re-entry is invalidated by the rule against perpetuities, and A gets a legal and equitable fee simple fee of the condition. This does not mean that all rights of re-entry are invalidated by the rule against perpetuities. If the condition were limited to A's lifetime, *e.g.*, "providing that A never uses the premises for the manufacture, sale or consumption of alcohol" the condition could be broken and the right of re-entry vest within A's lifetime but not beyond, and thus not violate the rule against perpetuities.

**43. P grants to L for life and then to A in fee simple subject to A's agreement to enroll in the Faculty of Law.**

P: legal and equitable fee simple in reversion if A has not agreed to enroll in the Faculty of Law by end of L's life

L: legal and equitable life estate

A: legal and equitable fee simple in remainder if A has already agreed to enroll in the Faculty of Law (assuming that condition is certain enough to be enforceable)

**44. P grants to A for 999 years to the use of B in fee simple when B is 21.**

P: balance of lease of equitable interest for 999 years by way of resulting trust, subject to divestment when B is 21; legal and equitable reversion in fee simple at end of A's 999 year lease

A: lease of legal interest for 999 years

B: lease of equitable interest for 999 years subject to condition precedent of reaching age of 21

**45. P grants to A for life, then to A's son, B, for life, then to B's widow for life, then to the use of A's grandchildren and their heirs who reach the age of 21.**

P: legal and equitable fee simple in reversion which vests in interest at the effective date of the grant and vests in possession on termination of the last of the prior particular estates

A: legal and equitable life estate

B: legal and equitable life estate which vests in interest at effective date of grant, and in possession on death of A

B's widow: legal and equitable life estate which vests in interest and in possession on death of B (cannot ascertain B's widow until B's death)

A's grandchildren: nothing

The grant of the fee simple to the grandchildren violates the rule against perpetuities. No grandchild can reach the age of 21 more than 21 years after the death of its parents, but as A is still alive, the common law presumes that she is capable of having more children. Thus, A's children are not relevant lives in being, as the class of A's children could include children born after the effective date of the grant. That leaves A as the relevant life in being, and, as it is possible for one of A's grandchildren to reach the age of 21 more than 21 years after the death of A, the grant to the grandchildren fails.

Small changes in the facts or in the wording of the grant would save the grant to the grandchildren. For example:

**(a) make sure that the holder of the prior particular estate is a life in being**

The grant is subject to the legal remainder rules, under which an interest must vest, if at all, during or at the moment of termination of the prior particular estate. **If** there were no prior particular estate to B's widow, but only to B, the class would close at B's death, and those grandchildren who had reached the age of 21 during B's lifetime would share in the fee simple, with those who were still under 21 being cut out. But the prior particular estate here is given to B's widow, who will not be ascertained until B's death, and who could be a woman who was not alive at the effective date of the grant. So although the class of eligible grandchildren closes on the death of B's widow, that is not necessarily within 21 years of the death of some life in being.

**(b) make sure that the widow is a life in being**

The grant to the grandchildren would be valid **if** B were dead at the effective date of the grant, because then his widow, if any, would be an ascertained person and thus a life in being. Alternatively, naming the widow by name rather than identifying her by her relationship to B would make her a life in being. As this is a grant of a legal remainder, the legal remainder class-closing rule would close the class within the time permitted by the rule against perpetuities, on the death of the holder of the prior particular estate. So long as that person must necessarily be a life in being, all possible vesting must occur within 21 years of the death of a life in being, which is the time permitted by the rule against perpetuities.

**(c) make sure that the children are lives in being**

The grant to the grandchildren would be valid, too, **if** A were dead at the effective date of the grant, because then there is no possibility of A having more children, and so A's children would count as lives in being. Since no child can reach the age of 21 more than 21 years after the death of its parent (plus the gestation period), no child could meet the condition precedent beyond the period permitted by the rule against perpetuities. If A is alive at the effective date of the grant, one could achieve the same result **if** one identified the class of grantees as A's grandchildren born to the children of A who are living at the effective date of the grant. With this class of potential grantees, all interests would have to vest during the lifetime or within 21 years of the death of the grantee's parent, and as that parent must, by the terms of the grant, be a life in being, that is within the period permitted by the rule against perpetuities. With either of these possibilities, the class would close on the termination of the prior particular estate, because of the legal remainder rules, perhaps cutting out some potential grantees, but at least the grant would be effective for those who meet the condition within the lifetime of the holder of the prior particular estate.

**(d) make sure that the class of grandchildren will include only those children who can meet the condition within 21 years of the death of a life in being at the effective date of the grant**

**If** the grants were only to B's children, rather than to all of A's grandchildren, the grant would be valid. As B is a relevant life in being, no child of B's could meet the condition of being 21 more than 21 years after the death of a relevant life in being. Alternatively, identify the grantees as the grandchildren of A born within the lifetime of the longest-surviving of A's children who were alive at the effective date of the grant. So long as the grandchild is alive before the death of the longest-surviving of A's children who were alive at the effective date of the grant, the grandchild has to meet the condition of reaching the age of 21 within 21 years of the death of that person. Of course, as this is a common law grant, subject to the legal remainder rules, the class would close at the end of the prior particular estate, and only those grandchildren who had met the condition at that date would share in the grant.

**46. P grants to A for life, then to A's children then surviving for life, then to the use of A's grandchildren and their heirs who reach the age of 21**

P: legal and equitable fee simple in reversion

A: legal and equitable life estate

A's children: legal and equitable life estate for those children surviving at A's death

A's grandchildren: nothing

The grant to A's grandchildren violates rule against perpetuities. Because A is alive at the effective date of grant, she could have more children, so A's children are not relevant lives in being, because children born after the effective date of the grant could join the class. The legal remainder rules would apply to the grandchildren's remainder, but that will not save the grant from the rule against perpetuities, because the holders of the prior particular estate are not necessarily lives in being. **If** A were dead at the effective date of the grant, or **if** the grantor had named A's children, rather than identifying them by a class description, or if the grantor had defined the class as A's children living at the date of the grant, the grant to the grandchildren would be valid.

**47. P grants to A for life, remainder in fee simple to those of A's children surviving at A's death.**

P: legal and equitable fee simple in reversion if A has no surviving children on A's death

A: legal and equitable life estate

A's children surviving at A's death: legal and equitable remainder in fee simple to those of A's children alive at A's death

There is no problem here with the rule in *Shelley's Case*, as the grant is to specific children who meet a condition, not to the whole line of issue. Nor is there a problem with rule against perpetuities. A is a life in being and the interests of children must vest, if at all, at A's death, because of the legal remainder rules.

**48. P grants to A for life, remainder in fee simple to those of A's children who visit A's grave once a week every week for the entire year after A's death.**

P: legal and equitable fee simple in reversion

A: legal and equitable life estate

A's children: nothing

The timely vesting requirement of the legal remainder rules applies to void the grant to the children *ab initio* because the condition for vesting cannot be met within or at the moment of termination of the prior particular estate. Note, though, that the verb "to visit" is used in the future tense, creating the possibility of an argument that the grantor intended to give the children a qualified fee simple which would vest immediately, but determinable or defeasible if the children failed to make the required visits to the grave. In that case, P would retain either a possibility of reverter or a right of re-entry for condition broken.

**49. P grants to A for life, remainder in fee simple to those of A's children who reach the age of 31.**

P: legal and equitable fee simple in reversion if none of A's children reach the age of 31 during A's lifetime

A: legal and equitable life estate

A's children who reach age of 31 during A's lifetime: legal and equitable fee simple in remainder

A's children who reach age of 31 subsequently: nothing

The timely vesting requirement of the legal remainder rules closes the class of eligible children at the termination of the prior particular estate.

**50. P grants to T Ltd. in trust for A for life, and one year after A's death to convey the property to those of A's children and their heirs who visited A's grave once a week every week for the entire year after A's death.**

P: equitable executory interest in fee simple by way of resulting trust if none of children meet condition

T Ltd.: legal fee simple

A: equitable life estate

A's children who meet condition: equitable executory interest in fee simple

The corporation obtains a fee simple without using the words of limitation to create a fee simple. The grant of legal title to the corporation avoids the *Statute of Uses* and the legal and equitable interests separate. The legal remainder rules do not apply to equitable interests, so the built-in gap between the end of the life estate and the vesting of the children's interest does not invalidate the grant to the children. Nor does the rule against perpetuities, because the children's interest must vest, if at all, one year after A's death, and thus within the period permitted by the rule against perpetuities. Use of the past tense for the verb "visited" clarifies that visiting the grave is a condition precedent for the child's interest to vest.

**51. P grants to T Ltd. in trust for A for life, then in trust for those of A's children and their heirs who reach the age of 31.**

P: equitable executory interest in fee simple by way of resulting trust

T Ltd.: legal fee simple

A: equitable life estate

A's children: nothing

A is alive at the effective date of the grant and could have more children, so the class of children cannot count as lives in being. A child born after the effective date of the grant could reach the age of 31 more than 21 years after the death of A, which would be beyond the period permitted by the rule against perpetuities, so the grant is void ab initio. The grant to children would be valid if the age for vesting were 21, not 31.

**52. To T in fee simple on trust for A for life, then on trust for those of A's children and their heirs who reach the age of 31.**

P: legal executory interest in fee simple if none of A's children meet the condition

T: legal fee simple for scintilla of time

A: legal and equitable life estate

A's children who reach age of 31 during A's lifetime: legal executory interest in fee simple

A's children who reach the age of 31 subsequently: nothing

Under the rule in *Purefoy v. Rogers*, the legal remainder rules apply to legal executory grants that could take effect as legal remainders. There is no built-in gap in seisin with this grant to the children, so the grant is not void *ab initio* and the timely vesting rule applies to close the class at A's death. As A is a life in being, that means the children's interests must vest, if at all, during or at the moment of termination of the lifetime of a life in being and so within the period permitted by rule against perpetuities.

# GLOSSARY

This glossary does not provide exhaustive definitions, only meanings appropriate to the context. For a full account of the historical development and current meaning of these words, consult a good reference book, such as *The New Oxford Companion to Law*, Peter Cane & Joanne Conaghan, eds. (Oxford and New York: Oxford University Press, 2008).

***ab initio.*** from the beginning.

**aboriginal title.** right of First Nations' collectivities to use and occupation of land, based on their ancestors' use and occupation of those lands prior to European assertion of sovereignty; one of a cluster of aboriginal rights protected by s. 35 of the *Constitution Act, 1982*; sometimes called native title.

**aboriginal rights.** rights of First Nations' collectivities, including right to aboriginal title, based on use of natural resources and use and occupation of land prior to contact with Europeans, or, for aboriginal title, prior to European assertion of sovereignty.

***ad medium filum aquae.*** to the middle thread of the water; the boundary between lands of riparian owners on opposite banks of a non-tidal river.

**adverse possession.** occupation of real property without permission of person holding title, which, if continued for time defined in relevant limitations legislation, may defeat rights of title holder.

**alienation.** voluntary sale or other disposition of interest in property, *inter vivos*, or by will.

**beneficial interest, beneficial title.** interest in property of person entitled to full rights of ownership recognized and enforced by a court of equity; also called equitable interest or title.

**bequest.** gift in a will, generally referring to a gift of personal property.

***bona vacantia.*** goods not claimed; property that belongs to the Crown because there is no one with claim to it, such as the personal property of persons dying intestate and without next-of-kin.

***cestui que usent*, also *cestuis que trust* (singular — *cestui que use* or *trust*).** persons entitled to beneficial interest in property, the legal title to which is held on trust.

***cestui que vie.*** measuring life for life estate *pur autre vie*.

**chattel real.** leasehold interest in land.

**chattels.** tangible property; goods.

**colour of title.** mistaken, but reasonably held, belief that one has legal title.

**commutation.** transmutation of legal obligations into another form.

**condominium.** form of ownership of residential or commercial real property combining individual ownership of parts of the property with co-ownership of other parts.

**constructive trust.** trust imposed by judicial decision on the title holder of property to remedy the wrongdoing of the title holder or to prevent his or her unjust enrichment.

**contingent.** conditional on the happening of some future event; not vested.

**conveyance.** transfer of freehold or leasehold estate by instrument; any instrument effecting a conveyance.

**covenants.** promises or agreements in writing under seal.

**Crown.** Queen or King for time being; in constitutional monarchy, used as substitute for word "state" to personify rights, duties and prerogatives of sovereign; in Canada, federal government or government of provinces or territories.

***cuius est solum, eius est usque ad caelum et ad inferos.*** who owns the fee in the surface, owns not only that surface but up to Heaven and down to Hell.

**curtesy.** right of widower to life estate in all real property of which wife solely seised at her death if a child born of the marriage.

**deed.** document under seal, signed and delivered, transferring interest in property.

**defeasible.** liable to being cut short on specified happening.

**determinable.** coming to an end — whether by limitation, flow of time, merger or otherwise.

**devise.** grant of real property by will.

**dower.** right of widow to life estate in one-third of real property of which husband solely seised at any time during marriage.

**easement.** non-possessory interest that owner of estate in land may have in nearby land of another, such as right-of-way across neighbour's land, or right to drain water across neighbour's land.

**emblements.** growing crops annually produced by the labour of the cultivator.

**equity.** body of principles and rules developed by Chancellors of England and Courts of Chancery and now applied by combined courts of law and equity.

**equitable interest, equitable title.** interest in property recognized and enforced by a court of equity, sometimes called beneficial interest or title.

**equity of redemption.** right of mortgagor to regain title to mortgaged property by paying amount owing; difference between the value of property and mortgages and other charges against it.

**escheat.** in modern common law jurisdictions, process whereby property reverts to Crown in right of province if owner dies intestate and without next-of-kin as specified in intestacy legislation.

**estate.** rights and obligations in land that make up ownership, defined by length of time that rights and obligations exist.

**execute.** (1) to sign, seal and deliver a deed; (2) to convert an equitable estate into a legal estate by operation of the *Statute of Uses*.

**executory interest.** an interest in property that may vest in the future, other than a remainder or reversion.

**expropriation.** taking of interest in land by government or other entity acting pursuant to statutory authority for public purpose authorized by statute.

**family property.** general term for various categories of property that are defined in provincial or territorial legislation as property subject to division between partners on marriage breakdown, and, in some jurisdictions, on death of a spouse; terms used in legislation include matrimonial property or marital property.

**fee.** legal estate in land, other than a leasehold, that is capable of being inherited.

**fee simple.** most extensive freehold estate in land; inheritable, with potential to last forever.

**fee tail.** freehold estate in land that is inheritable and lasts as long as there are children born in the direct line of succession.

***feme covert.*** a married woman.

***feme sole.*** a single woman.

**feoffee.** grantee in a conveyance; one who acquires seisin by a feoffment.

**feoffment.** transfer of title to real property, initially possible only by livery of seisin.

**fiduciary relationship.** relationship in which one party has rights and powers that must be exercised for benefit of other party; relationship in which party in position of power and confidence with respect to another must act in utmost good faith to protect interests of other.

**fixtures.** articles attached to the land or a structure on the land so as to become part of the land.

**frankalmoign.** form of feudal tenure in England whereby ecclesiastical bodies held land in return for saying prayers and masses for the soul of the grantor; not subject to feudal incidents.

**freehold.** estate in property with indefinite termination point.

**grant.** creation or transfer of rights and obligations in property; general term including transfer by gift or sale.

**grantee.** person who receives grant; transferee.

**grantor.** person who makes grant; transferor.

**gratuitous.** given voluntarily — for no reward, recompense or consideration.

**homestead legislation.** legislation in four western Canadian provinces protecting family home from seizure by creditors or from being transferred without consent of spouse.

***in capite.*** in chief.

***in personam.*** personal.

***in situ.*** in place.

***in specie.*** in a specific form; physical property rather than its monetary equivalent.

**incidents.** obligations owed to lord by tenants, arising on happening of specified events such as death of tenant.

**incorporeal hereditament.** non-possessory interest in another's land, capable of being transferred; either *profits à prendre* or easements.

**instrument.** formal legal document.

***inter vivos.*** while living; between living people.

**international law.** customary law and treaties governing conduct of independent states in relations with one another.

**intestate.** without valid will.

**joint tenancy.** form of co-ownership in which owners have equal shares in property, equal rights to possession, and *jus accrescendi.*

***jus accrescendi.*** in joint tenancy, right of remaining owners to receive share of deceased owner; also called right of survivorship.

**knight service.** main form of feudal tenure, subject to feudal incidents; abolished by *Tenures Abolition Act* in 1660.

**law French.** Anglo-Norman language used in English courts even after 1400, when French no longer used generally in England; abolished by statute in 1733.

**leasehold.** estate in land for defined term, also called chattel real.

**legal interest.** interest in property recognized and enforced at common law.

**lessee.** a person who holds the lease of a property; tenant.

**lessor.** the person who grants a lease; the party to a lease contract who provides the asset and receives the lease payments; landlord.

**licence.** non-proprietary right to do something on land of another that without licence would be trespass.

**life estate.** freehold estate in land that will last for the lifetime of the grantee.

**life estate *pur autre vie.*** life estate that will last for life of named person, called *cestui que vie.*

**limitation.** term in grant that defines duration of estate or interest granted; see also "determinable" and "words of limitation".

**limitation period.** period set by statute within which to bring a civil claim; expiry of a limitation period normally provides a defendant with a procedural defence to the claim.

**livery of seisin.** ritual to transfer title to estate in land (while on land, grantor hands grantee a clod of earth, tree branch or other physical symbol of estate in land, while saying words of grant, then departs).

**merger.** incorporation of lesser estate in greater.

**mortgage.** security interest in property, typically involving transfer of title to creditor until debt is paid.

**mortgagee.** lender who provides money on the security of a mortgage; creditor under a mortgage.

**mortgagor.** borrower who provides security for the loan by giving a mortgage to the lender; debtor under a mortgage.

**mortmain.** literally, the dead hand; describes legislation limiting conveyances to corporations or charities.

**native title.** *see* aboriginal title.

***nec vi, nec clam, nec precario.*** without violence, without stealth, without permission: describing quality of use necessary to acquire easement by prescription.

**operation of law.** coming into existence of legal consequences on happening of certain events without further acts of parties.

**paraphernalia.** clothing and personal ornaments that wife brought with her to the marriage or that husband gave wife during the marriage, which remained her separate property.

**particular estate.** freehold or leasehold estate less than a fee simple.

**partition.** ending co-ownership of land held by joint tenants or tenants in common by division of land into individually owned parcels.

**perpetuity.** contingent future interest that is void because of possibility that may vest beyond perpetuity period.

**perpetuity period.** period permitted for vesting by Rule Against Perpetuities; life in being plus 21 years.

**personal property.** also called personalty; all property other than freehold estates and other interests in land except leaseholds.

**presumption of advancement.** presumption that, in certain relationships, gratuitous transfer of property or purchase of property in name of another intended as gift of property.

**presumption of resulting trust.** presumption that gratuitous transfer of property or purchase of property in name of another creates trust relationship, whereby person holding title does so for benefit of grantor or person who paid for the property; a resulting trust for benefit of grantor arises in conveyance to uses of fee simple in which grantor has not named beneficiary of entire beneficial interest.

**primogeniture.** rule of inheritance whereby one's property on death goes to eldest son.

***profit à prendre.*** right to enter land of another to take products of soil or portions of soil itself.

**public policy.** indefinite set of moral values invoked by judges to invalidate conditions that they consider contrary to public order or good; for example, undue restraints on marriage or provisions to encourage separation of spouses generally held to be against public policy.

***Quia Emptores.*** statute passed in England in 1290 prohibiting subinfeudation and permitting alienation of land *inter vivos* without lord's consent; contributed to concentration of all feudal lordships in Crown.

***quicquid plantatur solo, solo credit.*** that which is attached to the soil becomes part of the soil.

**real action.** lawsuit brought for recovering of specific property.

**real property.** also called realty; estates and interests in land, both legal and equitable, except for leaseholds.

**received law.** case law and legislation that is transferred from a colonial power to a colony at the time of acquisition by settlement.

**reception, date of.** date for determining the law that is received into a colony; all relevant statute and case law as of the date of reception becomes part of the law of the colony.

**remainder.** legal estate in land that goes to remainderperson at termination of prior particular estate: vested remainders are present interests, even if they are not vested in possession.

***res ipsa loquitur.*** the thing speaks for itself.

**restraints on alienation.** conditions that prevent or limit the sale or other disposition of interest in land.

**resulting trust.** trust that arises by operation of law, when a grant in trust does not dispose of the entire beneficial interest; with a voluntary conveyance of property to a third party, in the absence of proof of gift; or where one person contributes the purchase money for property but title is held by another, again in the absence of proof of gift.

**reversion.** estate in land arising by operation of law whenever grantor grants a particular estate without granting the fee simple to a remainderperson; what grantor retains during particular estate; vested reversions are present interests, even if they are not vested in possession.

**riparian.** on the bank or shore of a body of water that flows in defined channel.

**riparian rights.** rights of holder of fee simple in land bounded or crossed by a river or stream to make use of water from the river or stream.

**seisin.** right to immediate possession of legal freehold estate in land.

**soccage.** form of non-military feudal tenure, not subject to incidents; remains as only form of tenure in Canadian common law jurisdictions.

**sovereignty.** supreme power in defined territory; ultimate power to determine law in, control and administer defined territory.

**subinfeudation.** transfer of some of rights and obligations of estate ownership from tenant to subtenants in which tenant retains some rights and obligations, thereby adding another layer to feudal triangle; prohibited by *Quia Emptores*.

**sui generis.** in a class by itself; unique.

**tenancy in common.** form of co-ownership in which owners have equal right to possession of whole property but not necessarily equal shares in estate; no *jus accrescendi*.

**tenement.** describes properties affected by easements; dominant tenement benefits from easement and servient tenement is burdened by easement.

**tenure.** terms and conditions on which one holds an estate in land.

***terra nullius*.** land of no one.

**testator.** person making a will; person who dies leaving a valid will.

**treaty rights.** rights confirmed in binding agreements between First Nations collectivities and Crown.

**trust.** relationship in which holder of legal title to property holds property for benefit of others, called beneficiaries or *cestui que usent*; essence of trust is separation of legal and equitable ownership.

**trustee.** person who holds title to property not for his or her own benefit but on trust for beneficiary of trust.

**use.** mediaeval term for trust.

**vested in interest.** describes present interest in property, for which grantee has met all conditions of eligibility, although right to possession may be deferred until expiration of some prior estate.

**vested in possession.** describes present interest in property in which grantee entitled to immediate possession.

**vesting.** point at which interest intended for someone becomes that person's property; moment of vesting in interest may precede moment of vesting in possession.

**waste.** conduct that permanently alters the nature or value of real property.

**words of purchase.** words in grant that identify person who is to take an estate or interest in land by the grant, whether by purchase or by gift.

**words of limitation.** words in grant that define duration of the rights and obligations being granted, thereby defining estate or interest being granted.

# INDEX